The New Crusade

The New Crusade

AMERICA'S WAR ON TERRORISM

Rahul Mahajan

MONTHLY REVIEW PRESS

New York

Copyright © 2002 by MONTHLY REVIEW PRESS
All Rights Reserved

Library of Congress Cataloging-in-Publication Data
available from the publisher.

ISBN: 1-58367-070-X paperback

MONTHLY REVIEW PRESS
122 West 27th Street
New York, NY 10001

Printed in Canada

10 9 8 7 6 5 4 3 2

CONTENTS

CONTENTS

INTRODUCTION

The world changed on September 11. That's not just media hype. The way some historians refer to 1914–1991 as the "short twentieth century," many are now calling September 11, 2001, the real beginning of the twenty-first century. It's too early to know whether that assessment will be borne out, but it cannot simply be dismissed.

On that day, 19 terrorists wielding knives hijacked four passenger planes, crashing two of them into the twin towers of the World Trade Center in New York and a third into the Pentagon. Shortly thereafter, both towers collapsed. Passengers in the fourth plane attacked the hijackers, causing them to lose control of the aircraft, which went down in rural Pennsylvania. The total death toll was over 3000, including citizens of over 80 countries. Over 350 of the dead in the World Trade Center were firefighters, who charged into the buildings to assist people inside in making their way down.

As the nation reeled in shock at this unprecedented event, the FAA grounded all passenger flights and military aircraft patrolled the skies over New York and Washington, D.C. The borders were closed, and the White House was evacuated. Around the country, people came together in solidarity, rushing to give blood. In lower Manhattan, closed to most traffic, shoe store clerks gave sneakers free to high-heeled women unequipped to walk. Instead of athletes, musicians, or actors, the heroes that all paid tribute to were the firefighters who lived in obscurity until called to risk and give their lives to save others.

The attacks occasioned a chorus of condemnation around the world. Yaser Arafat of the Palestinian Authority said, "We are completely shocked. It's unbelievable. We completely condemn this very dangerous attack, and I convey my condolences to the American people, to the American president and to the American administration, not only in my name but on behalf of the Palestinian people." Cuban Foreign Minister Felipe Perez Roque said, "Cuba laments and expresses its profound sadness for the loss of so many innocent lives and expresses our absolute rejection of acts of terrorism, wherever they may come from." Mohammad Khatami of Iran said he felt "deep regret and sympathy with the victims." And even Wakil Ahmed Mutawakil, the Taliban's foreign minister, told the Arab television network al-Jazeera, "We denounce this terrorist attack, whoever is behind it." The only world leader not to join in was Saddam Hussein of Iraq.

The attack was a crime against humanity, and it seemed all humanity realized it. For a brief moment, the community of nations was realized in shared grief and outrage—the phrase of the hour, echoed around the world, was "Today, we are all Americans."

The attacks of September 11 forever ended the idea that the United States could somehow float above the rest of the earth, of it and not of it at the same time. Americans can no longer foster the illusion that what happens to the rest of the world doesn't affect them. It is more crucial than ever that we understand what kind of world we are living in, and what the United States has done to make it so. That is something that can be agreed on by the entire political spectrum, even if there is disagreement on where the blame lies.

The amount of information that one must process in order to understand everything that's going on has already multiplied beyond belief. In order to keep from losing the reader in a welter of confusing facts, and because there is as yet little historical distance, many important but secondary questions must be left aside. This book focuses on three main questions:

— What measure of truth is there in the version of events and their causes and consequences that is conveyed by the U.S. government and the mainstream media?

— What is the larger historical context in which the war on terrorism can be understood and assessed?

— What can we expect to happen next, now that the military conquest of Afghanistan has been completed?

In Part One, I try to frame the discussion by examining point by point the official view of the war on terrorism that has emerged and is being pushed on the public. In Part Two, I examine aspects of U.S. foreign policy over the past decade or more, and put forward the idea of a "new white man's burden"—a drive to make a new kind of cultural supremacism (generally expressed in universalist terms but no less supremacist because of that) an element of U.S. imperial ideology and an essential part of the war on terrorism. In Part Three, I discuss possible developments in the regions most likely to be targeted for further action in the war on terrorism and in the United States itself.

In all of these tasks, I try to develop this analysis with as few presuppositions as possible. The discussion is distinguished from a mainstream analysis by the following points:

— I assume that the history of U.S. policy, especially the recent history, is relevant to understanding what is being done today — the common dodge is to use the "change of course" doctrine to suggest that, no matter what was done wrong in the past, things are very different now.

— I do not ignore facts just because they have been given little or no media coverage.

— I do not assume the benevolence of the U.S. government. I do assume, however, that the easily predictable consequences of actions taken by the government were in fact predicted by government planners, and that, therefore, the government is culpable and should be held accountable for them.

The analysis I have given relies only on such a minimal analytical framework. In fact, of course, I bring to the enterprise a much broader framework, which informs the discussion at various places.

To have any chance of dealing with the problem of international terrorism, we must change the role of the United States in the world. In an essay entitled "The War Comes Home," published on the Web the day after the attacks, I wrote, "The main practitioner of attacks that either deliberately target civilians or are so indiscriminate that it makes no difference, is no shadowy Middle Eastern terrorist, but our own government." These attacks run the gamut from direct bombing, as the United States has done in Iraq (on numerous occasions), Serbia, Sudan, Afghanistan, and other countries in the past ten years alone, to denying people access to the basic necessities of life. From the sanctions on Iraq, which have for years involved denying basic medical care to millions, to efforts to keep South Africa from providing affordable AIDS drugs to its citizens, the United States has killed countless civilians.

There is always a justification, as there is for any killing anywhere — for the sanctions on Iraq, it is the security of Iraq's neighbors and for denying AIDS drugs it is the need to maintain corporate profits. For the terrorists who attacked on September 11, it was the need to oppose U.S.-sanctioned murder and oppression in their part of the world. If "terrorism" is to be given an unbiased definition, it must involve the killing of noncombatants for political purposes, no matter who does it or what noble goals they proclaim.

When Madeleine Albright, then secretary of state, went on *60 Minutes* on May 12, 1996, Lesley Stahl said, referring to the sanctions on Iraq, "We have heard that a half- million children have died. I mean, that's more children than died in Hiroshima. And, you know, is the price worth it?" Albright, not contesting the figure, replied, "I think this is a very hard choice, but the price—we think the price is worth it." That is the philosophy of terrorism. The people who crashed planes into the World Trade Center killed almost 4000 people because they resented U.S. domination of the Middle East. The U.S. government helped to kill 500,000 children in Iraq in order to preserve that domination.

It is the common fashion to dismiss such juxtapositions as claims of "moral equivalence." In fact, that concept is irrelevant. Whether or not the U.S. government is "morally equivalent" to the terrorists, whatever that might mean, the point is that citizens of the United States have a particular obligation to oppose its crimes. This does not mean efforts should not be made to stop terrorists of the ilk of Osama bin Laden. It means that terrorist efforts to stop them should not be made. The war on Afghanistan has been even worse—terrorist in its methods and designed primarily to project U.S. imperial power, not to address the problem of terrorism.

If Albright or any other architect of U.S. global policy appears on *60 Minutes* again, they should also be asked whether they think U.S. policy goals in the Middle East were also worth the deaths of thousands of Americans.

Note: All dates in this book are in 2001, except where the year is otherwise indicated.

Part One

THE WAR ON TERRORISM —
MYTH AND REALITY

1. Another Pearl Harbor

To those familiar with the history of U.S. policy, the immediate question occasioned by the attacks of September 11 was, "Who's going to get it — and how bad?" In the absence of an overwhelming oppositional movement, war was inevitable from the first moment. TV anchors started the drumbeats of war within hours of the tragedy, speculating ceaselessly on the same questions — which countries should be targeted, and be reduced to rubble. In his first speech to the nation, President Bush said, "We will make no distinction between the terrorists who committed these acts and those who harbor them." His statement was interpretable only as a threat to attack some country since "harbor" could potentially mean — as, in fact, it did end up meaning — people who happen to live in the neighborhood of the terrorists even if they had no knowledge of, interaction with, or influence over the actions of the terrorists.

In the days to come, the theme of vengeance and extreme violence in retaliation cropped up numerous times. Senator John McCain, speaking in Congress on September 12, addressing the terrorists, said, "God may show you mercy. We will not." The following day, at a Defense Deptartment briefing, Deputy Secretary of Defense Paul Wolfowitz spoke of "ending states who sponsor terrorism" (he did later correct himself and claimed that he was misunderstood).

The most frequently used comparison was with the Japanese attack on Pearl Harbor. Lance Morrow of *Time* magazine (September 14) invoked the analogy, writing, "A day cannot live in infamy without the nourishment of rage. Let's have rage. What's needed is a unified, unifying, Pearl Harbor sort of purple American fury."

In some ways, the analogy doesn't go far enough — Pearl Harbor was part of a colony annexed by the United States less than 50 years before, not, as New York and Washington, D.C., the economic and political centers of the country. And the attack was on a military base (although there was no declaration of war, the United States was engaged at the time in a partial blockade, an oil embargo, and constant harassment of Japanese shipping, usually considered acts of war), not on a civilian target.

In other ways, the analogy was overwrought. Japan was a state with a powerful economy and a powerful military, that had the ambition and the means to control and exploit southeast Asia, while the perpetrators of the attack were 19 men, part of a network with at most a few thousand hard-core militants and access to modest financial resources. While it was clear that they could wreak destruction on U.S. soil in an unprecedented manner, their dispersed nature and modus operandi justified and suggested a cautious, careful and highly selective approach in dealing with them. They were not about to take over the world, and options other than war could easily have been explored.

It's not difficult to surmise that the invocation of Pearl Harbor was a way to galvanize the nation, assert that the danger to the world was similar to that posed by the Axis in World War II, suggest that the retaliation on yet unnamed targets should be as severe as it was in that war, and imply that Americans had to try to measure up to the Greatest Generation in moral fiber. In the same article mentioned earlier, Morrow added, "Let America explore the rich reciprocal possibilities of the *fatwa*. A policy of focused brutality does not come easily to a self-conscious, self-indulgent, contradictory, diverse, humane nation with a short attention span."

In a similar vein were the numerous invocations of Neville Chamberlain's concessions to Hitler in Munich (where he accepted Hitler's annexation of Czechoslovakia), always in response to any antiwar arguments. It had a powerful emotive force, because of the obvious fact that capitulation then had meant that the eventual war with Germany was far more destructive. For similar reasons, the same analogy was repeatedly used when Saddam Hussein invaded Kuwait, even though Hussein had neither the capability nor the will to invade any other countries. The analogy was also strained by the fact that no one in the antiwar movement or elsewhere advocated appeasement.

2. They Hate Us for Our Freedom

Although no one claimed responsibility for the attack, it was immediately and widely conjectured that Middle Eastern terrorists were involved. After the Oklahoma City bombing, numerous media anchors and antiterrorism "experts" had made fools of themselves speculating about Oklahoma City as a hotbed of Islamic fanaticism. Once again, within hours, reports that a group of

Arabs was responsible were widespread—but this time it seemed to be true as the passenger lists of the planes became public and Arabic names appeared in groups of four and five.

For weeks after the attack, the question "Why do they hate us?" reverberated through the country. It was not a question asked during the Vietnam War, the Gulf War, or any of a series of American engagements, because none of them involved attacks on America, and in those cases the hate seemed almost exclusively directed the other way.

George W. Bush, in this as in all else, got people on the wrong track in his first speech to the nation—"America was targeted for attack because we're the brightest beacon for freedom and opportunity in the world." Others rushed to jump on the same bandwagon. Sen. Charles Schumer (D-N.Y.) in congressional session the next day, said "They hate us for our freedom." In the days to come, it became a constantly repeated mantra, expressed by talk-show hosts, actors, and people on the street. Many acted as if even questioning the idea was prima facie evidence of mental deficiency.

It was a nice, comfortable idea. Throughout the 1970s and early 80s, when it was clear to Americans that most of the world was "anti-American," it was generally easier to believe that the reason must be envy of Americans' wealth, freedom, and overall success than to consider questions of America's role in the world. As anti-Americanism around the world seemed to abate in the 90s, it became easier to believe that those still holding to it were simply pathological.

Dan Rather summed up the instinctive American evaluation of this phenomenon on CNN's *Larry King Live* (October 18). Asked, "Why do they hate us," his response included this gem of wisdom—"They hate us because they are losers. They see us as winners. And those who see themselves as losers sometimes develop a deep and abiding hatred for those they see who are winners. There is a lot of—there is some envy from around the world." He concluded, "And, frankly, there are just evil people in some places. And evil can't be explained."

Such ideas dovetail perfectly with the American penchant for easy answers as well as easy demonization of non-white Third World peoples, especially of Arabs, who have long been the last group it is respectable to feel prejudice against. The fruits of centuries of this urge to excommunicate from humanity whoever happens to be the foe at the moment are clear. Political phenomena in human societies are now inexplicable, to be ascribed simply to unknowable primal urges—if they depart from the dominant framework of our society.

And yet, perfectly rational reasons to oppose the United States were never hard to find. It was certainly predictable, though unfortunate, that these reasons translated into hatred. The foundations for anger and resentment in the Third World were laid starting right after World War II. At the time, the United States was perceived as a proponent of decolonization and so was relatively popular throughout the colonized world. This started to change when it was seen that it was more interested in shifting colonies from the spheres of various European powers into its own. The CIA coups in Iran in 1953 and Guatemala in 1954, the destruction of Vietnam from 1954 to 1973, interventions in Brazil, the Dominican Republic, Laos, Cambodia, Chile, Angola, Nicaragua, and more all had much to do with anti-Americanism around the world. The obvious rejoinder to any mention of this history, often made by people who opposed those interventions but supported war this time around, is that none of those people ever attempted to carry out an act like the WTC attack.

Even so, whatever considerations were in the mind of Osama bin Laden or members of his network, his broadcast statements contain no mention of any resentment of American democracy, freedom, or the role of women. There was no need for conjecture about the reasons that al-Qaeda targeted Americans. In fact, several news reports mentioned al-Qaeda's recruiting video, used to take raw recruits and instill in them hatred for America. The propaganda points in that video have to do with U.S. domination of the region, not with the internal organization of American society.

Among the many images in the video is one of Mohammed al-Durra, the 12-year-old child killed by Israeli army fire early in the Palestinian people's al-Aqsa intifada, which started on September 28, 2000, with Ariel Sharon's visit to the Haram al-Sharif, or Temple Mount, in Jerusalem. The photo of him dying in his father's arms was shown around the world, arousing horror at Israeli state violence. Other photos included pictures of Iraqi babies dying of malnutrition in underequipped hospitals, victims of the U.N. sanctions, which have been in place since August 6, 1990, and were estimated by UNICEF to have killed 500,000 children under the age of 5 by the end of 1998, in addition to an uncounted but perhaps roughly equal number of adults and children over 5.[1] Although the sanctions are multilateral, they are being held in place by the United States—all but a handful of countries have turned against them.

Interestingly, the one event with non-Muslim targets included in the video is the nuclear bombing of Hiroshima. Although most American have long since accepted the facile rationalization that the bombing saved not just American lives but Japanese lives because of a purported fanatical desire of

Japanese to fight to the death if invaded, the rest of the world was generally unable to swallow such a grotesque claim. The fact that the story has been conclusively refuted by analysis of declassified documents[2] has not, unfortunately, been covered in the American media or in high school history courses. In fact, Japan was willing to surrender, as long as the emperor was left unharmed—the United States had broken their code long since, and was aware of all high-level diplomatic correspondence. In the event, the United States, while insisting on unconditional surrender, ended up preserving the emperor as a bulwark against Communism. The most likely reason for the atomic bombing was to send a message to the Soviet Union—perhaps 300,000 innocent people were sacrificed to send that message.

If people happened not to read about the recruiting video, the first video-tape of bin Laden, released after the United States started bombing Afghanistan, repeated the mentions of Hiroshima, Palestine, and Iraq.

One does not have to be sympathetic to bin Laden's twisted and reactionary ideology to share resentment against the sanctions on Iraq and Israel's occupation, which is undertaken with the aid of several billion dollars a year in U.S. military aid (the tanks, helicopter gunships, artillery shells, and F-16s with which the Israeli army attacks civilian populations in the occupied territories are made in the United States). Those grievances are widely held in the Islamic world.

Unfortunately, those who suggested even the possibility of legitimate grievances were repeatedly condemned as apologists for terrorism—even though virtually every article or speech that talked about underlying reasons began with a condemnation of the atrocities of September 11. Nobody in the antiwar movement said anything that remotely justified the killing of civilians. Quite the opposite, people often get involved in antiwar movements precisely because of deeply held convictions about preserving life.

The reactions to the horrible events of September 11 were split. Even as a significant minority woke up to the fact that U.S. foreign policy was relevant to them and hungered to learn more, encouraged by the administration and the media, the majority reflexively hid their heads in the sand. The unconscious sentiment always prevalent in the United States, that we don't have to think about such matters, rose to a conscious level in the collective backlash against the mere idea of studying U.S. policy as a guide to recent events. Amidst the clamor, one columnist summed it up perfectly: "Why do they hate us? They hate us because we don't know why they hate us."[3] To which one can add, "And because even now they don't want to learn."

3. You're with Us or You're with the Terrorists

The collective drive for revenge and against understanding gained momen-
tum with George Bush's address to a joint session of Congress on September
20, one of the most important presidential speeches in living memory. For
over a week everyone had been saying that our world changed on September
11. In a sense, however, it was on September 20 that the world changed, the
day that Bush announced the American jihad. The speech is worth dwelling
on, since it lays out so many fundamental principles of the war on terrorism.

Amidst the talk of revenge and annihilation, the world had been holding
its collective breath to see what would be the tone of Bush's first major, pre-
planned, policy address. Would it continue in the same vein or strike a more
conciliatory note?

The speech garnered much praise, with Bush generally described as states-
manlike, restrained, and even eloquent. Eric Alterman, a regular columnist
for *The Nation* and nominally on the left, commented in a column posted on
MSNBC within an hour of the conclusion, "The president appeared to hit virtually every note just right. He was not overly belligerent, and did not play up
to jingoist sentiments," praising him also for his "stirring eloquence." Joining a
sycophantic chorus, he even praised Bush for paying tribute to the firefighters
and other heroes of the rescue efforts and for calling for an end to hate crimes
against racial and ethnic minorities (not exactly controversial moves).

Alterman's column was broadly representative of the reaction from around
the country and, to a lesser extent, around the world. And yet the speech
required no exacting exegesis to discover a message of polarization and resolve
on destruction. Identifying (without releasing any evidence) Osama bin
Laden's al-Qaeda organization as responsible for the attacks, Bush made the
following demands of the Taliban:

> Deliver to United States authorities all the leaders of al-Qaeda who hide in your
> land. Release all foreign nationals, including American citizens, you have unjustly
> imprisoned. Protect foreign journalists, diplomats and aid workers in your
> country. Close immediately and permanently every terrorist training camp in
> Afghanistan, and hand over every terrorist, and every person in their support struc-
> ture, to appropriate authorities. Give the United States full access to terrorist train-
> ing camps, so we can make sure they are no longer operating.

While some of the requirements were understandable, others were of the
kind that no sovereign state would allow of another. No talk of extradition —

just a demand to "deliver" an unspecified number of unnamed individuals. No request for assurances from the Taliban of nonaggression — just a demand for them to allow another country "full access" to sensitive sites. Just to make sure there was no possibility of agreement, Bush added, "These demands are not open to negotiation or discussion. The Taliban must act, and act immediately. They will hand over the terrorists, or they will share in their fate."

Perhaps the most disconcerting of the demands was to turn over every person in the terrorists' "support structure." What is a support structure? Presumably, it includes cleaners and servants and those who deliver food, in addition to drivers, bureaucrats, and many others. The warning that the Taliban must obey completely or share the fate of the terrorists was in a similar vein, and not calculated to evoke conciliation.

Bush went on to say that the newly christened "war on terror" would not end until every "terrorist group of global reach" was stopped, an ill-defined and deeply inequitable statement, given that "terrorist group" was clearly going to be defined in such a way as to include the terrorism of the weak but exclude the terrorism of the powerful. He warned that "any nation that continues to harbor or support terrorism will be regarded by the United States as a hostile regime."

What exactly is meant by "harboring"? Emanuel Constant, one of the thugs involved in organizing FRAPH, the Haitian paramilitary group that supported the military coup by killing thousands of civilians and terrorizing countless others, walks the streets of New York a free man. Scores of Cuban-Americans involved in terrorist acts against Cuba are being "harbored" by the U.S. government.

Former Secretary of State Henry Kissinger, accused of war crimes and crimes against humanity in connection with Vietnam, Cambodia, Chile, East Timor, and numerous other places, is not only free but a highly respected "elder statesman" who regularly gives commentary on news and political talk shows when he has time from his busy schedule of working to get U.S. corporations sweetheart deals from repressive foreign regimes. When in Paris recently, he was asked to give testimony in connection with the Pinochet trials, but he ignored the request. He is currently being sued for his connection with the assassination of General Rene Schneider, a prelude to the coup in Chile. Recently declassified documents show that he and President Ford were fully aware of Indonesia's planned invasion of East Timor (they were in Jakarta right before it happened) and not only assented but gave advice as to how its impact on public opinion could be minimized — in addition to supplying

Indonesia with the arms to carry out its genocidal campaign, which killed 250,000 East Timorese (almost one-third the population).[4]

Warren Anderson, former head of Union Carbide's India operation, is wanted for corporate malfeasance that led to the deaths of nearly 15,000 people from cyanide poisoning. Even though India has made a formal extradition request, with documentation, the United States has made no move to extradite him. Because the United States has made it clear since that speech that harboring terrorists is sufficient reason for a country to be bombed, presumably there is no objection to Cuba, Haiti, and other countries bombing the United States.

The core of Bush's speech was contained in the line, "Every nation, in every region, now has a decision to make. Either you are with us, or you are with the terrorists." Like his father before him, Bush was declaring a "new world order." Independent policy and middle ground were a thing of the past. In this new world, a nation or a group could not condemn both terrorism and the U.S. response to it—such concepts would have no meaning. Collective punishment was no longer an aberration but the norm—entire peoples could legitimately be devastated because of the presence of a few criminals among them. Most important, the world was deliberately polarized, divided into two armed camps. Like Bush Sr.'s new world order, this one has not been realized yet, but the mere declaration is frightening enough.

After the United States started bombing Afghanistan, the preplanned release of a recorded video by Osama bin Laden offered a bizarre counterpoint to Bush's pronouncements. Bin Laden's statement was a broadcast call to the *ummah*, the Muslim world, denouncing the United States for the bombing of Hiroshima, the support of Israel's occupation of Palestine, the sanctions on Iraq, and the general domination of the Middle East, and then saying "these events have divided the world into two camps, the camp of the faithful and the camp of infidels."

Speeches about American foreign policy made by politicians are generally incomplete without at least one claim that God is on our side—"Freedom and fear, justice and cruelty, have always been at war, and we know that God is not neutral between them." Any irony in mirroring the claims of fundamentalists, in representing what was supposed to be the great battle of civilization against theocratic fanaticism in terms entirely acceptable to such a fanatic was, strangely, lost on Bush and much of the American public.

That it was more than a passing reference can be seen in the initial plans, since aborted, to give this "crusade" (a term dropped by Bush at a press briefing—presumably he was unaware that, although the term is understood in a de-historicized sense in the United States, that is not so in the Islamic world) the name "Operation Infinite Justice." With its repellent air of fundamentalist Christian eschatology, of Armageddon and the Rapture, the term was one of the most terrifying aspects of a very terrifying situation (in deference to the objections of Muslim clerics—and many others—who complained that infinite justice was something best left to a higher power, the name was later changed to "Enduring Freedom").

I wrote at the time, "The Pentagon planners are not speaking of justice spread infinitely throughout the world. Instead, it is 'justice' ad infinitum—to the end. The war of the 21st century begins now. It is justice by the sword. It ends in victory not peace, and Bush has made it clear that the sword will be unsheathed for a long time to come."

The ominous implications of that worldview are all too clear when, in a Defense Department briefing on September 18, Defense Secretary Donald Rumsfeld said, "We'll have to deal with the networks. One of the ways to do that is to drain the swamp they live in, and that means dealing not only with the terrorists, but those who harbor terrorists." The phrase "drain the swamp" has roots in Mao's description of a guerrilla army as a fish swimming in the sea of the people. U.S. counterinsurgency experts after World War II took up the phrase in the concept of "draining the sea" to counter guerilla warfare—a strategy carried out in South Vietnam by massive bombing, forced evacuation (the strategic hamlet program), deforestation (11 million gallons of Agent Orange were dropped in Vietnam), and large-scale torture and political repression (the Phoenix program).

No sooner was the phrase uttered than it was on everyone's lips, from government officials to newspaper editorials around the world. The logic of extermination, of killing ten innocent people to catch one guilty one, of assuming all who didn't support the extermination were themselves guilty, was all in place. How it played out in practice would depend on how much force was sufficient, not on any consideration of principle.

4. Self-Defense

And yet, even while claiming the right to do as it pleases, because it has the power, the U.S. government seemed very attuned to considerations of principle. While announcing its intent to violate international law, human rights, and abstract principles of justice, it simultaneously mounted a campaign to claim that its contemplated actions were not just entirely legitimate but the only possible response of right-thinking people. For example, from the beginning, the United States claimed that any attack, anywhere, at any time that they might launch would be justified as self-defense under international law.

The United Nations Charter is not only the primary document of international law, binding on all signatories (i.e., members of the United Nations), as a treaty ratified by the Senate it is the highest law of the United States as well. Chapter VII of the Charter is the section concerning the use of force. It is quite explicit that all use of force, with one exception, must be done by decision of, and under the aegis of, the Security Council, the 15-member governing body of the United Nations, which includes five nations—the United States, Russia, the United Kingdom, France, and China—as permanent members with the power to veto any resolution.

The only exception is for self-defense, mentioned in Article 51 of the Charter, which states in part, "Nothing in the present Charter shall impair the inherent right of individual or collective self-defense if an armed attack occurs against a Member of the United Nations, until the Security Council has taken measures necessary to maintain international peace and security." To a majority of the American people, this seemed clear enough—we were attacked on September 11 and we had the right to strike back.

In an interesting sidelight, several columnists took pains to distinguish this war from other postwar military campaigns—the war on Afghanistan, like World War II, was a necessary war, not optional like Vietnam or the Gulf War. As Charles Krauthammer put it in the *Washington Post*, "Half-measures are for wars of choice, wars like Vietnam. In wars of choice, losing is an option. You lose and still survive as a nation."[5] This casual acceptance of the fact that the United States had violated international law and committed aggression in every war it has fought between World War II and now (the U.N. Charter requires that war be a last resort, after every other option has been tried) was quite remarkable, and obviously done only to strengthen the case for self-defense in this particular case, relying on historical amnesia to make past cases irrelevant.

The criteria for self-defense are a little more stringent, however, than they were generally represented to be. The internationally accepted standard dates from the so-called Caroline incident in 1837, when the British attacked the USS *Caroline*, which was trading with rebels against British rule. In Secretary of State Daniel Webster's formulation, an attack can be considered self-defense if the "necessity of that self-defense is instant, overwhelming, and leaving no choice of means, and no moment for deliberation," adding that responses must be neither "unreasonable" nor "excessive." In other words, for military action to be self-defense, there must be an imminent threat of attack, there must be no alternative available in time, and even then it must be targeted specifically at those who pose the threat.

The attack on Afghanistan met none of those criteria. It happened almost four weeks after the initial attack, easily enough time to make arrangements for the Security Council to deal with the problem. As we will see later, if the goal was extradition of bin Laden and accomplices, there was an alternative, left deliberately unexplored — negotiation with the Taliban on the basis of presenting evidence, as is generally expected in extradition cases. And the response was directed against Afghanistan, even though none of the 19 hijackers were Afghan and there is no evidence known of even a single case of an Afghan being involved in terrorist attacks on the United States.

Furthermore, Afghanistan, unlike the United States, has no long-range bombers or intercontinental ballistic missiles, nor any other way of striking at the United States. In fact, if there was an imminent threat of attack, it came from terrorists either already in the United States or likely to be in transit to the United States, and such a threat could hardly justify bombing any foreign country.

At a more basic level, many people used the analogy of a situation in which a maniac has broken into your house and already killed one family member — do you negotiate with such a person or shoot to kill? The obvious implication was that the antiwar movement was stupid enough to negotiate in a situation where only immediate self-defense made sense. The analogy to U.S. action would have been more accurate if the maniac had died in the attack, and your response was to bomb a neighborhood he had been staying in, killing many people who didn't even know of his existence — even though you had your own police force constantly on the watch for more attacks.

To cover the complete emptiness of this claim of self-defense, some claimed that the United States had already obtained the necessary authorization from the Security Council. And it is true that the Security Council passed two resolutions before the bombing started, 1368 on September 12 and 1373 on September 28.

Security Council Resolutions are of two kinds, those that authorize the use of force to enforce them by invoking Chapter VII of the Charter, and the so-called optional resolutions that are theoretically binding but do not authorize force. Resolution 1368 is of the latter kind, condemning terrorism and the attacks of September 11, calling on all nations to enforce past resolutions concerning terrorism, and stating that the Security Council will remain "seized of the matter," meaning that it is under constant review. In the preamble clauses, which have no legal force, it, oddly, "recognizes the inherent right of individual or collective self-defense in accordance with the Charter." Seemingly a redundant repetition of well-understood rights, it's more likely that the wording is there to muddy the waters—it does not claim that any specific action by any specific state against another is actually self-defense, but the United States government can always state that it does. Wording of this kind is often fought over fiercely, even when it seems irrelevant to the uninitiated.

Resolution 1373 is a Chapter VII resolution, authorizing the use of force. Passed by unanimous vote, it requires nations to take several concrete steps against terrorism—to criminalize fund-raising for terrorists or affiliated organizations, to prohibit people or entities within their borders from making funds available to such groups, to suppress recruitment for terrorist organizations, among others. It also mandates creation of a committee of the Security Council to monitor compliance with the resolution, requiring states to report their efforts to it within 90 days. Nowhere does it authorize the use of force by any given state against any other.

In fact, no Security Council resolution ever has. The UN Charter requires that use of force, except for self-defense, be carried out under a Military Staff Committee with representatives from different nations, and under the auspices of the United Nations—a requirement that the United States did not comply with even in cases where some use of force was authorized, like the Gulf War. And yet it was convenient to obfuscate the truth, and make it look as if the United States had been building international support for its war.

5. Multilateralism, Diplomacy, Restraint

Before September 11, the Bush administration had set off on a very openly unilateralist course, withdrawing from the Kyoto Protocols on global warming, pushing National Missile Defense in violation of the ABM treaty with Russia, scrapping proposed enforcement measures in the Biological and Toxin Weapons Convention in favor of unilateral U.S. enforcement and, of course, the favorite pastime of recent presidents, illegally bombing Iraq.

In the weeks after the attack, many pundits posited the notion that U.S. policy had shifted to multilateralism—if true, a positive development. *Arms*

Control Today (October) had an article entitled "The End of Unilateralism?" and an Australian columnist (Alan Dupont, *The Australian*, October 3), went so far as to claim that "the unilateralism that characterised the early months of the Bush administration has given way to a more collegial multilateralism."

Commentators pointed to several pieces of evidence. In addition to the aforementioned use of the Security Council to pass resolutions against terrorism, there was the expedited passage through the House on September 24 of a bill authorizing payment of $582 million in unpaid UN dues. The background to this was years of U.S. refusal to pay its back dues, an offense for which any other country would face expulsion from the General Assembly. It had also made it clear that payment of dues was contingent on reduction of the legally mandated U.S. contribution to the UN from 25 percent to 22 percent of the total budget — a clear violation of the UN Charter, which does not allow individual states to dictate terms to the UN.

Another indication was NATO's invocation of Article Five of the so-called Washington Treaty, its founding document, which stipulates that an attack on one NATO member is an attack on all and can be met with military force under the rubric of collective self-defense, a right guaranteed by Article 51 of the Charter. Beyond all of that was the feeling projected of patient diplomacy used to assemble an international coalition — supposedly something like the Gulf War coalition. In truth, U.S. policy was as unilateralist as ever.

Part of the problem is the definition of multilateralism in mainstream American political discourse, aptly encapsulated in a statement made in 1994 during Security Council deliberations about Iraq by then Secretary of State Madeleine Albright, "We will act multilaterally when we can, unilaterally as we must." The U.S. view of multilateralism is that it is merely a convenient device, to be used if it can be but always with the underlying threat that unilateral action will be taken if approval is not gained. Of course, this vitiates the essence of the term. A true multilateralist would try to gain international support for its planned course of actions, but would also abide by adverse international decisions.

Even if other countries wished to sign on to U.S. policy, the underlying element of coercion — the clear implication that the United States will carry out its intended policy whether sanctioned or not — means that any agreement by other countries is never really free. And, in fact, the United States applies a whole raft of mechanisms to exert direct pressure on countries. Most of them stem from the incredible economic dominance of the United States, which is far in excess of its share of the world's GDP. It effectively controls the World

Bank and IMF, even though it does not technically have a majority of the votes, and it is the one country that can impose genuinely harmful unilateral trade sanctions. Partly through the penumbra of that dominance and partly through its overwhelming military might, combined with extreme willingness to use it, it also has disproportionate political power.

The authorization to use force against Iraq in 1991 was passed through a combination of diplomatic browbeating, bribery, and coercion. The Soviet Union got a World Bank loan and China got restoration of diplomatic relations, terminated after the Tienanmen Square incident, as well as a $114 million loan for economic development. Yemen, which voted against the authorization, lost $70 million in development aid from USAID. Egypt got $7 billion in loan forgiveness. In general, other countries have learned the perils of crossing the United States politically, and usually avoid doing so unless they have a specific individual interest in the issue. Thus, a yes vote on the Security Council often does not even signify genuine support from the government of the relevant country, let alone from its people.

The U.S. approach to multilateralism was much the same in the case of the war on terrorism. Because the attack hit so close to home, the rhetoric started out considerably more heated—if the Gulf War coalition was built by browbeating, bribery, and arm-twisting, it seemed as if this time countries were being lined up in front of a firing squad, then asked "Are you with us or against us?"

In those first few days, when no one was quite sure how severe the U.S. reaction would be, since nothing like this had ever happened before, very few countries felt they could demur, much less suggest an alternative course of action. The incendiary rhetoric coming out of U.S. political figures was not exactly reassuring. Afterward, things started to change, and there was a realization that generalized threats and fear-mongering might actually backfire. With all the talk about destroying countries, ending states, using nuclear weapons, and much else, the veneer of protecting human rights, upholding the rule of law, and other obfuscations promoted assiduously by the United States to justify aggression cracked, and naked rage and arrogance poured through. That Americans held American life to be far more important than the lives of foreigners was made uncomfortably clear. Not only people in other countries, but even many normally apolitical Americans were appalled.

Pakistan was a critical country in the U.S. drive to war. Creator and chief supporter of the Taliban, it was also the one ally the United States absolutely needed to bomb Afghanistan. Its internal political situation is perpetually volatile, with an extremely vocal fundamentalist minority, many of them involved in some way in the Afghan jihad in the 1980s, very much against anything that smacks of the West. The initial rhetoric, treating Pakistan as a potential enemy unless it capitulated, made military dictator Pervez Musharraf's position more difficult—if he was seen as slavishly following U.S. orders, it would give the fundamentalists more ammunition to attack him.

And so the United States abandoned its talk of destruction and absolute obedience and went back to its usual tricks. In order to gain Pakistan's support, it dropped the remainder of the unilateral sanctions it had placed on Pakistan (and those on India) in 1998 after the nuclear bomb explosions. In exchange for rights of overflight and stationing special forces in Pakistan, as well as to get Pakistan to abandon the Taliban, it offered a $1 billion aid package, along with attempts to get more significant debt relief (Pakistan has an external debt of $37 billion, of which $3 billion is held by the United States).

The final word on multilateralism was Rumsfeld's, with his frequent reference to "floating coalitions." In a Department of Defense briefing on October 18, he summed up, "From time to time, I see references in the press to 'the coalition'—singular. And let me reiterate that there is no single coalition in this effort. This campaign involves a number of flexible coalitions that will change and evolve as we proceed through the coming period."

In other words, there was no broad international support for the entire U.S. agenda. Instead, on any particular issue, countries that could be browbeaten into assisting would be. And on the war against Afghanistan, initially the only country supportive enough to be part of the coalition was the United Kingdom—a coalition of two, described in some propaganda leaflets dropped on Afghanistan as the "Partnership of Nations," presumably an attempt to evoke the World War II international alliance of nations against fascism. In case the point had not been driven home, Rumsfeld went on to add, "A month from now, I expect someone somewhere might report that a particular nation is not doing something or has stopped doing something, and the speculation could be 'Is the coalition coming apart or unraveling?' Well, let me make clear: No single coalition has 'raveled,' therefore, it's unlikely to unravel."

In fact, the United States chose deliberately to act without international sanction. It had already obtained a unanimous vote in the Security Council on a Chapter VII resolution (1373) requiring that states undertake a series of severe measures against terrorism, without even an attempt to define terrorism. It has tremendous resources of coercion at hand, as discussed before. It had, at least initially, the sympathy of the world. Given all this, it is not hard to surmise that the United States could have squeezed authorization for military action out of the Security Council, but it chose not to.

The reason, publicly stated by Rumsfeld in the aforementioned briefing, was that "the mission determines the coalition, and the coalition must not determine the mission." In other words, the United States asserts the right to predetermine the mission, whether or not there is international support for it, a right it would never allow any other country to exercise in the international arena. Or, restated, the Bush administration wanted to make it clear that the United States does not consider itself bound by international law—it recognizes no higher authority than itself. Multilateralism, U.S.-style.

It must be said that, even though weak states can often be coerced and cajoled into acceptance of U.S. domination, this serves only to further alienate the people of those countries, exacerbating the risks to the United States in the long term.

Related to the "new multilateralism" was the idea that, in the nearly four weeks between the terrorist attack and commencement of the war on Afghanistan, the administration exercised "restraint" while it practiced "diplomacy."

In part, the talk of restraint was complete nonsense. Military operations on the significant scale of the Afghanistan war cannot be implemented overnight. Troops and materiel take time to move into place, especially when delicate negotiations are needed to establish bases in countries where such a move can have domestic political costs. The need for such bases was all the more crucial since Afghanistan is entirely landlocked, the worst kind of target for the typical high-tech U.S. bombing campaign. After some dithering, on September 30, Saudi Arabia indicated that no attacks on Afghanistan could be launched from there. It took time to secure the cooperation of Pakistan and of Uzbekistan, whose Termez airbase was a vital staging area for the U.S. operation. The buildup to the Gulf War lasted five months. No matter how tough their talk, Pentagon planners and their civilian chiefs do not make large-scale plans for military operations based on rhetoric. Words of war are spoken for public relations, not planning purposes.

There was also a genuine political question. In the press, it was presented as a debate between Secretary of State Colin Powell and a school centered on Rumsfeld, that included Deputy Defense Secretary Paul Wolfowitz, Richard Perle, and others. The debate took many forms—at one time, Powell said that evidence of bin Laden and al-Qaeda's involvement with the attacks would be made public, only to be brought up short by Bush, at another time it was over negotiation versus attacking, and throughout it was about whether or not to widen the war by targeting other countries, especially Iraq. To what extent this was a genuine debate and to what extent a good cop–bad cop scenario (even conservative commentator George Will suggested that some of it might be, in his words, "disinformation to confound our enemies") is difficult to determine.

There was a real question, however. How would the Islamic world react to different courses of action and how much power could the United States exert and still remain in control? Many analysts, especially on the antiwar side, tended reflexively to liken the situation to the Gulf War. And there were obvious similarities — an initial act of aggression that necessitated some response, the United States attacking a Muslim country, the need to placate or enlist other Muslim countries, and talk of building an international coalition.

There was, however, one key difference that created a world of difficulty for U.S. officials. The Gulf War was in response to Iraq's invasion of Kuwait, another Muslim country. The act itself split the Islamic world. Most governments, whether or not they cared for Kuwait, could not accept the occupation of a sovereign nation. The people of the Arab world were also divided. Since the United States proposed to attack one Muslim country in order to defend another, the war could not be presented as an attack on Islam. In this case, however, the attack was made in the name of Islamic fundamentalism, and the proponents of war talked of crusades and infinite justice. The country to be attacked, however horrible its domestic policies might be, had never committed aggression against any other Islamic state, or, indeed, any other state. The populace of the entire Islamic world was and is against the war on Afghanistan. Although the majority of that populace is not fundamentalist (a misleading label, but commonly used) and the majority of fundamentalists are not as extreme as al-Qaeda, there were certain shared grievances (Israel's occupation, sanctions on Iraq, etc.) as well as the outlines of a shared worldview. On the other side was an arrogant superpower, one directly responsible for creating and propping up corrupt, undemocratic regimes in the Islamic world, which seemingly wanted to pick a fight with a defenseless nation out of sheer desire for revenge. Thus, whatever incentives the governments of those countries, which generally represent very different interests than the people, might have to go along with U.S. plans, if they went too far there was a serious risk of destabilization.

Early on, a few U.S. government policymakers seemed to seize opportunistically on the tragedy as a way to implement a maximum program, bending much of the world explicitly to the will of the United States. Developments in the Islamic world, especially the growing distaste for various U.S. government statements, made it necessary for U.S. planners at some point to step back, examine their approach, and change it, at least in superficial appearance. An appearance of restraint was necessary, in order to avoid further destabilizing potentially volatile situations in many countries, including Pakistan and Saudi Arabia, and to allow those governments to cooperate with the United States (to the extent they did) without appearing utterly craven.

There was no question of principle, however, no argument about how legitimate it was for the United States to dictate to other countries, much less a genuine restraint based on attempts at diplomacy. At best, it was a tactical maneuver designed to gain time and maximize what the United States could actually get away with.

If the above arguments seem to impute too much diabolical intent to the United States government, one need only examine the record of what is usually referred to as "diplomacy" regarding the extradition of bin Laden. Initially, the Taliban claimed that bin Laden could not have been directly responsible for the attacks, since the Taliban had cut off his communications with the outside world (it's known that bin Laden has avoided use of satellite phones for years, for fear that those transmissions could be traced and used by the United States to assassinate him). Shortly thereafter, they convened a *shura*, an assembly of Islamic clerics, of over 1000 mullahs who came from all over the country to decide the question of whether bin Laden would be turned over.

The *shura* could not make a firm decision either way, instead asking bin Laden to leave the country voluntarily—a sure sign of a political division that could have been played upon by a genuinely diplomatic initiative.

But, of course, diplomacy is predicated on negotiation. It is the political art of reconciling competing interests without a resort to violence. In this and similar situations, the United States generally eschews diplomacy from the beginning. In the prelude to the Gulf War, the constant refrain was "no negotiations," sometimes changing to "no linkage" when Saddam Hussein suggested a joint resolution of Iraq's invasion of Kuwait and of Israel's occupation of Palestine. Here again, the message, repeated ever since the September 20 speech before the joint session of Congress, was the same—"These demands are not open to negotiation or discussion."

Before attacking Serbia in March of 1999, the United States made demands of the government, at the village of Rambouillet, France, which amounted to requiring that Serbia allow a U.S.-led NATO military occupation of Kosovo. When Serbia refused to those terms, it was claimed that efforts at diplomacy had failed and all that was left was force.

Similarly, Bush's demands amounted to allowing indefinite U.S. military occupation of Afghanistan, couched in the language of offering the United States "full access to terrorist training camps." They also called for the Taliban to hand over an unspecified and potentially endless list of people to the United States, just on its say-so, including possibly people in the "support structure" of the terrorists who were innocent of any crimes.

As with Rambouillet, these are demands that no sovereign government can allow and keep its sovereignty — especially since the potential occupier, the United States, is so overwhelmingly powerful. To make peremptory demands deliberately set so high that they cannot be met, and then to foreclose on any possibility of negotiations is the antithesis of diplomacy, yet this process is regularly referred to in the U.S. media as diplomacy.

But the full story was even worse than this. Shortly after the *shura*'s decision, the Taliban government began asking for the evidence of bin Laden's involvement — standard in any extradition request. In late November, the U.S. government finished amassing evidence in a request to extradite Lotfi Raissi, an Algerian pilot suspected in connection with the September 11 attacks, from Britain. Even though the judge has indicated he may not comply, there is no talk of bombing Britain.

Although Secretary Powell had initially said that the evidence would be publicly presented, the Bush administration quickly decided otherwise. Tony Blair of Britain did release a document, which was largely a collection of unsourced claims, along with a few highly questionable conclusions, presented as facts — for example, one piece of "evidence" was the claim that "No other organization has both the motivation and the capability to carry out attacks like those of the 11 September." Very little of the evidence actually related to the September 11 attacks — mostly, it covered al-Qaeda's connection to the U.S. embassy bombings in 1998.

Jurists who examined the document quickly came to the conclusion that, while it might be sufficient to indict (if all the unsourced claims were taken at face value), it would in no way suffice to convict — indeed, an updated document released later begins with the caveat, "This document does not purport to provide evidence against Osama Bin Laden in a court of law."

Although some claim that the videotaped statements released by bin Laden after the bombing of Afghanistan commenced are an admission of guilt, that question is not the central one. It is, after all, clear that bin Laden created and funded al-Qaeda, helping to provide training to future terrorists, and that he has called on those terrorists and others, on numerous occasions, to kill Americans, including civilians. A more interesting question is why the United States did not present its evidence to the Taliban. If the offer to turn over bin Laden to foreign judgment once evidence was presented was a bluff, at the very least the United States could have called it.

Shortly before the bombing started, the Taliban offered to turn bin Laden over to a neutral third country, even without hearing the evidence—even to allow him to be tried under Islamic law in the United States.[6] A week after the bombing started, when the offers were reiterated, Bush's response was: "There's no need to negotiate. There's no discussion. I told them exactly what they need to do. And there's no need to discuss innocence or guilt. We know he's guilty."

The reason for the peremptory demands was indicated by a statement of Taliban spokesman Amir Khan Muttaqi reported on November 1—"We do not want to fight," Muttaqi told the Associated Press. "We will negotiate. But talk to us like a sovereign country. We are not a province of the United States, to be issued orders to. We have asked for proof of Osama's involvement, but they have refused. Why?" The conclusion that the Taliban were deliberately treated with disrespect so that it would be impossible for them to simply turn bin Laden over is inescapable.

If any doubts remain, they should be dispelled by a story that ran in the *Daily Telegraph* on October 4, reporting that a secret deal to turn over bin Laden had been agreed upon, but that it was scotched. A delegation led by Qazi Hussain Ahmad, the Pakistani head of the fundamentalist Jamaat-i-Isla-mi, had agreed with Mullah Omar that bin Laden would be taken to Pakistan, where, within the framework of Islamic law, evidence of his involvement would be placed before an international tribunal, which would decide whether to try him itself or hand him to the United States. Even though the proposal had bin Laden's approval, it was turned down by Musharraf of Pak-istan on the bizarre grounds that he could not guarantee bin Laden's safety—seemingly no longer a concern as U.S. government officials openly call for him to be killed rather than captured. That Musharraf could make such a decision without U.S. approval is unlikely in the extreme.

And so we are left with the conclusion that the United States deliberately made sure that bin Laden could not be turned over through diplomatic chan-nels, through negotiation, because that would deprive them of their primary *casus belli*. The Bush administration deliberately sought war, not peaceful resolution — again, a violation of the UN Charter, which requires the use of all means short of force before taking military action.

6. Power, not Revenge

This analysis implies that the U.S. government wanted war, and raises the question of why they wanted it. One popular misconception that even the antiwar movement fed into with its slogan "Justice, not Revenge," was that the motivation for the war was simple, bloody-minded revenge.

It is true that the majority of the American public did feel an entirely understandable though deplorable desire for revenge, so powerful that for some little distinction was made between the innocent of the Islamic world and the guilty. It is also true that government officials, and especially prominent media spokespeople, whipped up and fed those sentiments (calls for restraint came later, as strategic considerations).

It is not true that such sentiments are significant determinants of government policy. Governments are made of human beings, but they are not themselves human. They often use emotion — certainly the Bush administration capitalized on the people's desire for revenge to build support for their war — but they act for other reasons. There were concrete reasons behind the deliberate, premeditated drive to war, but they lay elsewhere.

Far and away the most important reason for the war is imperial credibility. For at least five years after it became clear that the United States could not "win" in Vietnam, if winning meant maintaining the corrupt semi-colonial dictatorship of South Vietnam in power, the bombing of Vietnam continued, even escalating. The reason given ad nauseam was "credibility."

To understand the concept, one must start with the fact that the United States is an empire. It is not like the Roman Empire, based on direct military occupation and exaction of tribute, nor like the colonial empires of the nineteenth century, with their elaborate administrative apparatuses. It is, nevertheless, an empire, maintaining its economy through the control and exploitation of the resources and labor of many other countries. In order to maintain and extend that control, purely economic mechanisms are insufficient — coups have been fomented and wars fought by the United States to create the current world economic system.

But empires never rule stably. There is always the danger of revolt in the provinces. That danger is vastly multiplied if one area is seen to revolt and get

away with it. In order to maintain itself, an empire must make an object lesson
of any would-be breakaway state. In the case of the United States, even though
economic domination is the primary reason for the empire, the need to maintain long-term stability sometimes necessitates military action that is not clearly related to economic concerns — clearly the expenditure of resources over
Vietnam by the United States was far greater than any potential gain to it by
bringing Vietnam into its economic sphere of influence.

Destroying one Vietnam keeps ten other countries in line. As author and
foreign policy expert Noam Chomsky frequently says, "If you want to know
what credibility is, ask any Mafia don." If you don't pay the money you owe,
Mafia enforcers will not just take your money, they break your legs so that
everyone knows the price of crossing them. In this case, the challenge was not
just to U.S. dominance over faraway areas, but to the very heart of the United
States. In order to maintain its status as the one, unilateralist, interventionist
superpower, the modern empire, the U.S. government had to attack something.

The second reason is the oil and natural gas of the Caspian basin and the
related question of U.S. military bases in the newly opening area of Central
Asia. The area's oil reserves are variously estimated at from 35–200 billion
barrels — since little exploration has been done, the lower figure is likely
wrong and the higher figure extremely speculative. By way of comparison,
Saudi Arabia has 24 percent of the world's proven reserves, with 260 billion
barrels. Caspian Sea oil is more costly to extract than that in the Middle East,
but it is also not under OPEC, so would help to limit the power of that organization, always a U.S. goal. Turkmenistan has the world's third largest
reserves of natural gas and others have deposits as well. U.S. corporations
have for years been in negotiations with Kazakhstan, Turkmenistan, and
other countries in the area.

Afghanistan's location between the Caspian basin and huge markets in
Japan, China and the Indian subcontinent gives it critical importance.
Pipelines running west from the Caspian basin into Eastern Europe are of less
significance, because demand in those countries is projected to be stagnant,
while demand in Asia will grow rapidly. There are three alternatives for piping
oil and gas to those Asian markets: a pipeline through Iran, the most natural
choice but prohibited to U.S. corporations because of U.S. trade and investment sanctions; a pipeline all the way to China, so long that it adds
significantly to the cost of oil; and one through Afghanistan and Pakistan to
the Arabian Sea. Of those states, Afghanistan is the one most potentially con-
trollable by the United States.

A U.S.-controlled client state in Afghanistan would give U.S. corporations great leverage over those resources of Central Asia. Just as in the Middle East, the United States does not seek to own all those resources, but rather to dictate the manner in which wells and pipelines are developed and used, to control prices for economic stability, and to control the flow of profits from those resources.

This conclusion is strengthened by several revelations that came out after September 11. In a story that the BBC[7] published on September 18, former Pakistani Foreign Secretary Niaz Naik said that he had been told in July of plans the United States had made to attack Afghanistan in the fall. And in their book *Bin Laden: The Forbidden Truth*, French authors Jean-Charles Brisard and Guillaume Dasquie claimed that the Bush administration deliberately blocked some terrorism investigations in the summer of 2001 while it negotiated with the Taliban over construction of an oil pipeline through Afghanistan (for which the Taliban wanted political recognition and economic aid). As the negotiations broke down in August 2001, Brisard and Dasquie quote a U.S. official as telling the Taliban, "Either you accept our offer of a carpet of gold, or we bury you under a carpet of bombs."

On the domestic front, the war increased the potential to push a radical right-wing domestic agenda, making it easier to expand police powers, restrict civil liberties, and increase the military budget.

The professed motivation of "getting" bin Laden and his henchmen is obviously one of some importance to the United States, and is being carried out assiduously as this is being written. The fact that it is at best near the bottom of the hierarchy of goals is clear because the easiest and most certain way of getting him, showing evidence to the Taliban in exchange for a trial in a neutral venue, was deliberately avoided. The manhunt for bin Laden may or may not result in his capture or death, but is certainly far less sure a method than a trial would have been. This war was and is about the extension and maintenance of U.S. government power, at home and abroad. Other motives are strictly secondary.

7. A Humanitarian War

As preparations for the military campaign were being completed, the Bush administration suddenly professed a startling new motive for bombing. In the weeks after the bombing, the expressions of rage and desire for revenge were dying down, partly because more and more people were learning about the truly pitiable state of the Afghan people, living in a country ravaged by saturation bombing, civil war, and several years of drought, with 6 million people dependent on international aid programs. As public opinion swung from lashing out toward "bombing Afghanistan with butter," the government responded brilliantly, taking that very sentiment and using it to justify war.

The argument, floated by unnamed government officials in the New York Times on October 4, went like this:

— The Afghan people are starving, so we need to do airdrops of food and other supplies.

— Planes doing the drops would be endangered by Taliban air defenses, so we need to destroy those defenses first.

— The Taliban air defense includes hundreds of portable, handheld Stinger anti-aircraft missiles, supplied by the CIA to the mujaheddin during the 1980s. To take out portable air defenses, wide-ranging bombing is necessary.

At a press conference on October 7, shortly after the bombing had started, Rumsfeld said, "The effect we hope to achieve through the raids, which, together with our coalition partners, we have initiated today, is to create conditions for sustained anti-terrorist and humanitarian relief operations in Afghanistan. That requires that, among other things, we first remove the threat from air defenses and from Taliban aircraft." To that end, in addition to its conventional ordnance, U.S. forces dropped 37,500 individually wrapped meals a day, two planeloads, mostly over northern Afghanistan.

Thus did the United States present itself as the ultimate exemplar of civilization, using careful precision bombing to target only its attackers, while showering the innocents of Afghanistan with largesse. But there were several problems with this story.

Experienced humanitarian workers always consider airdrops a last resort. They can be dangerous, they are wasteful, and, most important, without an on-the-ground distribution network, they are almost useless in getting supplies to those who need them the most. In Afghanistan, the problems with drops are complicated by the fact that Afghanistan is the second most heavily mined country in the world. There are an estimated 10 million landmines and other bits of unexploded ordnance (UXO), which have killed several thousand people, perhaps as many as ten thousand, since 1993. Food packets landing in minefields have led to at least several deaths.

More important, before September 11, roughly 5.5 million people were being helped by a wide variety of relief programs, run by the World Food Program (WFP), the UN High Commission for Refugees (UNHCR), the Food and Agriculture Organization (FAO), UNICEF, and a host of private aid agencies, including Oxfam, Christian Aid, and Save the Children. The WFP, for example, ran a bakery project in Kabul that supplied 36,000 families with bread, and employed 259 widows, women who would otherwise likely starve under the Taliban's draconian laws about working women.[8]

All of this changed after September 11. The bellicose rhetoric coming out of U.S. government officials caused many Afghans to flee the cities, exacerbating an already severe refugee crisis — as Julian Filichowski, director of the Catholic charity Cafod that works in Afghanistan, said, "even the threat of military action has made the humanitarian situation worse," creating tens of thousands of new refugees. Current estimates from the UNHCR are that there are 3.6 million Afghans outside the country and perhaps 1 million "internally displaced." With the threat of war, the Taliban informed relief agencies that the safety of workers could no longer be guaranteed, so all foreign relief workers were pulled out and aid operations came to a grinding halt. Not only the use of force, but even the threat of force, is a violation of international law — especially when it has such grave humanitarian consequences.

After a few weeks, relief operations had just resumed, and organizations were attempting to tackle the Herculean task of getting in enough supplies before winter, having lost several weeks already. Before they could get fairly started, the bombing commenced and activities were disrupted again — the WFP, for example, announcing that all convoys into the country had been suspended and advising their 350 employees in Afghanistan to stay home. Although convoys into the country and distribution soon resumed, for weeks they were at a small fraction of the amount needed.

Because of the threat and then the actuality of war, the UN Office for the Coordination of Humanitarian Affairs estimated that the number of Afghans dependent on aid would grow from 5.5 to 7.5 million. Simultaneously, the threat and then the actuality of bombing caused existing aid provision to be terminated for weeks, and then resumed at half the necessary level. Thus, the bombing that was supposed to create conditions for relief operations disrupted the provision of aid to millions of people in order to feed at most 37,500 people a day (and that contingent on perfect distribution). The U.S. armed forces' entire stock of 2 million meals would scarcely cover one day's needs for one-fourth of the people needing aid.

To add insult to injury, while the bombing sent doctors and other educated people running to Pakistan the food packets had within them antibiotics with instructions for use in English, for a populace the majority of which is illiterate even in its native language.

Humanitarian organizations saw clearly enough that the airdrops were just a sham, a cover for a war of aggression, and not something springing out of humanitarianism. Private British agencies, in the delicately restrained prose of organizations that must be seen as "non-political" in order to function, have said military action makes airdrops "virtually useless" as an aid strategy. Barbara Stocking, director of Oxfam, said all aid should be channeled through the UN "to be seen as impartial and separate from military action," adding, "Trucking of food is cheaper and is tried and tested."

The Nobel prize–winning group Doctors without Borders went further, denouncing the food drops as "military propaganda." Virtually all agencies were concerned that the association in the minds of Afghans of bombing with humanitarian aid would undermine their position—as Jean-Hervé Bradol, president of Doctors without Borders, said, "We do not want to be perceived as a part of the U.S. military campaign."

Even U.S. officials described the campaign as a combination of a humanitarian and a psychological operation (psy-op in the felicitous phrasing of the military intelligence establishment)—suggesting that more important than any actual effect on the Afghan people's condition was that they create the idea that the United States was there to help. In truth, as worldwide opinion recoiled from the cynicism and hypocrisy of food mixed with bombs, it became clear that if it was a psy-op it was directed at the American people.

The cynical use of humanitarian concerns by a government that couldn't care less about the plight of the Afghan people was made even clearer by later developments. As the bombing and its attendant disruption of aid continued for several inconclusive weeks, fear grew among many aid workers and UN officials that winter would set in, making many routes impassable and precluding distribution of aid to millions of people. Although some food was getting in, many truckers refused to risk U.S. bombing by crossing the border.

UNICEF predicted that because of the disruptions, 100,000 more children (over and above the already chilling under-5 mortality rate of 257 per 1000) would die in the winter, unless something was done very quickly. The number of adults who might die was not estimated, but surely considerable.

On October 12, UN Human Rights Commissioner Mary Robinson called for a bombing halt so that supplies could be trucked in, saying "It is a very, very urgent situation. It is very hard to get convoys of food in when there is a military campaign. . . . You have millions of people, they say up to 7 million, at risk. Are we going to preside over deaths from starvation of hundreds of thousands, maybe millions of people this winter because we did not use the window of opportunity?"

The next day, presumably under political pressure, she disavowed the call, but it was shortly echoed by UN Special Rapporteur on the Right of Access to Food Jean Ziegler, as well as, on October 17, a combined statement from a group of private aid agencies including Oxfam International, Christian Aid, Action Aid, and Islamic Relief. In that statement, they noted that UN food stocks within Afghanistan were down to just two weeks' supply (9,000 tons) and that at least two million people didn't have enough food aid to last the winter — and of those, 500,000 would soon be cut off by snow.

The U.S. government ignored those concerns. When several Islamic governments started making similar calls, adding that there should be no bombing during Ramadan, which started on November 15, one might have expected the government to pay some heed — especially when even Pervez Musharraf of Pakistan, America's most indispensable ally, did so. Instead, all government statements indicated the bombing would continue unabated.

U.S. policy made its lack of concern for vital humanitarian issues clear, but there were indications of something even more sinister. Dropping food mingled with bombs was not the only way in which the United States tried to politicize the question of aid. Early on, they made it clear that any food distribution plan should be carried out "in a manner that does not allow this food to fall into the hands of the Taliban," in the words of Richard Armitage, deputy secretary of state.[9]

Since the Taliban, as the men with guns, were hardly the ones in need of humanitarian aid themselves — as long as there was any food in the country, they would be fed — it is not unreasonable to assume that the real goal was to allow aid into non-Taliban-controlled areas while keeping aid from the population in Taliban-controlled areas, thus giving them an incentive to oppose the Taliban or simply to leave. Indeed, when asked to explain how Armitage's considerations could be realized, State Department spokesman Richard Boucher "suggested that food could be distributed in refugee camps and areas not controlled by the Taliban."[10]

Of course, the first principle of humanitarian relief is that it be impartial, that aid be given on the basis of need without any consideration of political agenda. In fact, tampering with aid on political grounds violates international law. Unfortunately, the United States government has quite a record of doing exactly that.

The sanctions imposed on Iraq before the Gulf War deliberately exempted food, as a necessity of life for civilian populations. Even so, the U.S.-run naval blockade and land-based interdiction was so severe that, between August 1990 and April 1991, only 10,000 tons of grain, the amount Iraq needed for one day, was allowed into the country.[11] A proposed shipment of baby food from Bulgaria was prohibited by the United States on the grounds that adults might eat it.[12]

One of the avowed goals of the U.S.-run contra war on Nicaragua was to destroy the food supply and give people a choice between starvation and rejection of the Sandinistas—that war also saw the U.S. government arouse international execration by using Red Cross markings on planes used to smuggle arms to the contras.

In the mere five weeks between the commencement of bombing and the massive withdrawal of the Taliban the United States carried out several acts that were highly suggestive of an attempt to impose starvation and suffering selectively as a means of political coercion.

The first time a Red Cross warehouse complex in Kabul was bombed, with precision bombs, the claim that it was a mistake was widely accepted. Within days, however, the exact same complex was hit again—even though, as Red Cross spokespeople pointed out, it was clearly marked with a large red cross and the location had been given beforehand to the United States to be put on their list of prohibited targets. Although widely reported as yet another, highly unexplainable, mistake, there was a report, on MSNBC (10/31), that a "senior U.S. military official told NBC News that the Red Cross warehouses were not hit by accident, saying they were bombed because Taliban troops had commandeered the food stored there." Military analyst William Arkin corroborated this report, saying "high-level" military sources told him that "the bombing of the Red Cross facility was both deliberate and justified"—even as other news outlets continued to report the bombing as a mistake.[13]

In the event, it transpired that Taliban troops had not taken the food, which was being used to feed 55,000 families headed by disabled people. On another occasion, a Red Crescent dispensary in Kandahar was hit, making a total of at least three hits on International Committee of the Red Cross (ICRC) facilities.

At a Pentagon briefing on October 24, this politicization was taken to new heights with the invocation of unnamed "sources" claiming that "there are reports that the Taliban might poison the food and try to blame the United States," according to Rear Admiral John Stufflebeem, deputy director of operations for the Joint Chiefs of Staff. He went on to warn Afghans receiving aid, "If it comes from Taliban control, they must be careful."

This was quite a remarkable statement; obviously, poisoning one's own populace is senseless. In fact, there was no reason to suppose the Taliban was planning anything of the sort and, it transpired, they were not. Shortly after the briefing, officials from the World Food Program expressed "surprise" at the allegations, with one saying "If they're talking about the food we deliver, there's not been a single instance that we know of in which the Taliban have tampered with it. Stolen, yes, but not tampered." The inference that this was a piece of disinformation floated by the Pentagon as a "trial balloon," then dropped because it was so clearly absurd and unbelievable, is a difficult one to avoid.

The common U.S. government practice of issuing disinformation in wartime is by now well known to the public, and we will look at cases regarding Iraq and Kosovo in later chapters. In the war on terrorism, there had by this time already been a case of disinformation uncovered — the government was forced to admit that initial reports that the hijackers had been planning to target Air Force One were false. Although these inferential arguments are hardly conclusive, they are at least suggestive, as well as being consonant with U.S. policy in the past.

The sudden retreat of the Taliban, beginning with the loss of Mazar-i-Sharif in the north on November 10, following with withdrawal from Kabul on November 13, and quickly to isolation in a small area centered around Kandahar, largely obviated any plans for serious use of food as a political weapon. The U.S. government no longer had anything to gain by preventing Afghans in Northern Alliance–controlled areas from being fed. It also soon transpired that it had no particular interest in helping them to be fed, even though it shared responsibility for their circumstances.

Earlier, the U.S. government had put off calls for a bombing pause by claiming that the best way to address the humanitarian situation was by removing the Taliban from power, suggesting that they were the primary impediments to the aid program. It is undoubtedly true that the Taliban interfered in small ways with humanitarian aid. There were numerous reports of theft, although the Taliban leadership promised to put an end to it. When the World Food Program resumed its convoys into Afghanistan several days after the bombing started, some Taliban officials attempted to tax them, not only a disgusting act but a violation of international law. Even before the crisis, the

Taliban had frequently made it difficult for aid agencies to operate, especially for women workers. But there was a great deal of spin involved in presenting this as the primary problem. As spokespeople for the normally nonconfrontational Christian Aid said, "The idea that the Taliban are systematically ripping off aid convoys is ridiculous," adding, "The whole military effort since 11 September is what has disrupted humanitarian relief. We have been working successfully with the Taliban for four or five years. While they didn't make things very easy we did get the job done."[14]

When the Taliban withdrew, there was a brief period of triumphalism—a quick "I told you so" delivered to the supposedly faint-of-heart who had called for a bombing halt—and then the issue of humanitarian aid was largely forgotten. Of course, the government had not predicted the quick withdrawal, saying even before it started that the campaign would probably last for months—thus, it was playing with the lives of 7.5 million Afghan civilians in an absolutely unconscionable manner.

Even worse, however, within weeks of the withdrawal, those who called for a halt were being vindicated. As the humanitarian crisis deepened, the U.S. government once again showed its militant lack of concern for the people whose existence it has endangered. As John Davison, a spokesperson for Christian Aid, summed up on November 21:

> There is a misplaced sense of relief and victory since the success of the Northern Alliance. The ironic truth is our ability to bring or distribute food in Afghanistan is not any better than it was during the bombing. The main routes we had managed to establish were coming in through Pakistan and lately virtually nothing is getting in I believe only a single convoy got in yesterday. With the frontline moving back and forth and the continuing infighting there is now more instability, which greatly hampers humanitarian efforts. Soon it will get to the point that the trucks won't go out at all because of fears of getting stuck in the snow. This the third year of the drought and the past two years the aid agencies had prepared for the winter by stockpiling supplies before the winter. By our normal schedule and we have done it twice before so we know what we are doing we should have been finished by now. Right now, things have hardly started. By all means, everyone is glad that the Taliban have mostly lost power but the recent developments have demonstrated the lifesaving importance of the pause in the bombing that we and with six other major international aid agencies had called for—our call went unheeded and now we face this crisis. In the Western and Central Highlands where we carry out most of our work, about 80 percent of the population is very vulnerable. Our workers on the ground report that food is very short

and people are trying desperately to get out and they have no means of transportation. That's hundreds of thousands of people facing starvation. Yesterday, an international conference discussed how to rebuild Afghanistan. We must first save their lives.

The Taliban's only virtue, and the primary reason they had some popular support, was that they brought order to the regions they governed. The so-called Northern Alliance, by contrast, is a group of warlords, all of whom have made and broken numerous alliances, often fighting on the side of former foes against former allies, then switching sides again. Many, like the Uzbek General Abdul Rashid Dostum, are corrupt as well as brutal. When the pre-Taliban mujaheddin factions were in the ascendant, from 1992 to 1996, the country saw chaos on an unequalled scale. An estimated 50,000 civilians were killed in Kabul alone, and the whole country was laid waste.

Although the Taliban interfered with aid, there was some control from higher up. Afterward, with a massive increase in banditry, the level of food aid getting in to the north, which was where Northern Alliance control was strongest, dropped to half what it had been during the war, before the Taliban withdrawal started—which itself had been much less than needed.[15]

Many aid agencies called for peacekeeping troops to help safeguard delivery and distribution of aid. The United States vetoed such plans repeatedly, even having a falling out with its closest ally, Britain, over Britain's plans to introduce 6000 peacekeepers. Clare Short, international development secretary of the British Labor cabinet, accused the United States of not taking the aid effort in Afghanistan seriously enough.[16] Only on December 5 did the United States even agree in principle to a peacekeeping force, although it put up enough procedural roadblocks that there was still not one on the ground by mid-December.[17]

Simultaneously, Rumsfeld said, of the ongoing manhunt for bin Laden, "There will be further casualties in this campaign in Afghanistan and elsewhere. We may have troops captured or killed." The inference that capturing bin Laden was a goal worth risking American lives, but that helping to feed Afghans displaced and subject to threat of death because of U.S. bombing was not, was inescapable.

U.S. ally Uzbekistan kept the so-called Friendship Bridge, which connects it with Afghanistan across the Amu Darya River, closed, severely hampering aid convoys that were concentrated in that area. The Bush administration was extremely dilatory in addressing this, with the result that it stayed closed until well into December, severely hampering aid efforts in the north around

Mazar-i-Sharif, in whose immediate vicinity 150,000 refugees are living in flimsy tents, completely dependent on aid.[18]

The extremely heavy U.S. bombing around Kandahar devastated the city, causing an estimated 85 percent of its 800,000 population to flee.[19] As of December 11, there had been no food or medical convoys into the city for over three weeks.[20] On December 6, Doctors Without Borders was forced to pull out of Jalalabad, an area which was being heavily bombed because of its proximity to the Tora Bora cavern complex, because, according to Georges Dutreix, the head of mission, "The feeling of the people (in Jalalabad) is changing a bit following the killing of the civilians," adding, "You don't need too many people to make the situation very dangerous. There are a small number of people there who are already anti-Western and when you have a situation like this, people can become very aggressive."[21]

The nearly two months during which almost no aid got through had many effects. Although the World Food Program was able to get enough food to meet the minimal needs of the at-risk population, it was initially unable to get the food to at least an estimated 1.5 million people, in severe danger of starvation.[22] According to the *Independent* (December 13), "One spokesperson from *Médécins sans Frontières* was quoted . . . saying that less aid was entering Afghanistan now than before 11 September."

In December, 116,000 tons of food, apparently enough to feed 6 million people for two months, was brought into Afghanistan. This occurred mostly through heroic efforts by the World Food Program and other organizations, which jumped to resume aid at the highest levels possible as soon as large-scale bombing ended. With the entry of this good, the World Food Program proclaimed that the danger of massive famine was over, although other organizations like Save the Children said the danger had simply been pushed back a few months and keeping it from recurring would depend on a steady flow of aid. At the same time as the problem in terms of gross tonnage was temporarily solved, numerous distribution problems continued to plague relief organizations right through the end of January.

Some areas were in danger because of their remoteness, which meant that they needed to get their aid before winter made many roads impassable. In early January, for example, there were reports that about 50,000 villagers in the mountainous region of Abdullah Gan were living mostly on bread made from grass, since bringing relief supplies from their nearest storage point was prohibitively difficult.[23] Also in early January came reports that the Maslakh (the name means "slaughterhouse") refugee camp near Herat, which had swelled from a pre-September 11 population of about 30,000 to over 350,000, was in critical condition, with an aid network unable to deal with the flood of new arrivals. It was estimated that 100 each day were dying of exposure and starvation.[24]

An explosion in corruption and misappropriation of supplies, as well as the already noted increase in banditry and theft of supplies, imperiled food distribution in the cities; often, after showing up to get aid, people would find that there were no supplies at the distribution points.

In addition, the Food and Agriculture Organization had been warning for months of a crisis in agriculture. Because the bombing had taken place precisely during the fall planting season, many farmers were unable to finish their planting, thus auguring potential famine in the spring. If humanitarian operations maintain their present high pace, the worst may still be avoided, but there will undoubtedly be significant propagating effects from the bombing for a long time to come.

In general, the American bombing campaign has been presented as a great humanitarian success, enabling a much larger flow of aid once the Taliban were destroyed. The truth is that, while the Taliban were in power, the United States pursued policies that greatly aggravated the existing humanitarian crisis, allowing significant amounts of aid through only after the Taliban left. The main obstacle to getting aid in in the critical period of mid-September through mid-November was the United States, not the Taliban. And the success in getting enough aid in after that period is largely due to the stepped-up efforts of international relief organizations, not to any special priority the United States put on relief operations.

8. Surgical Strikes

The other plank of the U.S. plan of aggression with a human face was the oft-repeated idea of "surgical strikes" using "smart" bombs. This claim has been made and discredited enough that even Peter Jennings of ABC, when first confronted with a military expert on October 7 talking about precision weapons, questioned him about the truth of those claims.

Still, the central point is not widely understood — there is no such thing as a surgical strike, at least with regard to U.S. bombing campaigns. In the Gulf War, for example, as audiences sat mesmerized by video of smart bombs destroying targets with pinpoint accuracy (with no human beings in them, or so it seemed), the truth was that 7.4 percent of the ordnance dropped was smart, and almost 93 percent was conventional "dumb" gravity bombs. Of those smart bombs, half missed their targets—overall, the rate of misses was 70 percent. In the war against Serbia, 29 percent of the total explosives were smart.

Technology has improved tremendously since then, but even in this latest war, the claims were merely that precision weapons hit their target 70–80 percent of the time, missing 20–30 percent. And right from the beginning non-precision weapons were being used as well—as of early December, according to the Pentagon, of 12,000 bombs dropped to date on Afghanistan 60 percent were precision-guided.[25]

More important, although there is much rhetoric of picking only military targets, the United States has a long record of deliberately attacking civilian targets. In the Gulf War, Iraq's electrical power generation and water treatment facilities were targeted, and nearly all of them destroyed. In the NATO war on Serbia, again, there was wide-ranging destruction of civilian infrastructure.

In this war, civilians were killed by precision weapons that accidentally went off target, by weapons that are by nature indiscriminate in their effect but were aimed at military targets, and, in some cases, by deliberate targeting decisions. The bombing campaign developed in a way fairly typical of recent U.S. interventions. Starting with a very narrow focus, targeting air defense and "command-and-control" centers, mostly with precision weapons, it gradually widened to attacks using a mixture of precision weapons, unguided bombs, and anti-personnel weapons like cluster bombs, on a wide array of different targets. As the small store of predetermined targets was exhausted, the country was divided into "kill boxes" (since renamed "engagement zones") where pilots were to attack "targets of opportunity."

From the beginning, targets located in the middle of civilian residential areas were attacked—for example, on the first day, the offices of the Defense Ministry in downtown Kabul. Given the 20–30 percent failure rate of precision munitions, this was a recipe for assured "collateral damage." Many targets were also picked on the basis of surveillance information obtained from the sky, without detailed on-the-ground knowledge, so that the number of civilians in the "military" targets on the list is unclear.

And, indeed, from early on, the reports began to mount up. On October 8, four UN de-miners who had remained when the rest of the staff was evacuated in order to serve the people of Kabul were killed when a smart bomb went astray. Amid much coverage rightly referring to the firefighters who charged into the World Trade Center as heroes, there was no reference to these unfortunate pieces of collateral damage as heroes.

Shortly thereafter, the village of Karam (Korum) near Jalalabad in south-eastern Afghanistan was hit by multiple attacks, with various claims of from 100 to 200 deaths as a result. Journalists who visited found at least 18 freshly dug graves, but could not confirm higher numbers (they were told the graves contained multiple bodies). When pressed about the casualties, Rumsfeld claimed that any dead in the village were killed by secondary explosions, the primary attack being on an ammunition dump in a cave complex near the village, adding, "I mean, let's face it, you do not spend that kind of money, and dig that far in, and store that many weapons and munitions that it would cause that kind of sustained secondary explosions unless you have very serious purposes for doing it. And the people in the vicinity clearly were connected to those activities."[26] Given his complete lack of knowledge of the activities of the villagers in question, his decision that none were civilians was stunning, but predictable in the way it echoes past U.S. military doctrine — free-fire zones in Vietnam and the declaration in the Gulf War that Basra, a city of 800,000, was "essentially a military target."

On October 22, the village of Chowkar-Karez was attacked. First came a wave of planes dropping bombs and then, as villagers ran out of their homes to avoid the bombs, they were repeatedly strafed with gunfire. All told, the attack lasted an hour. Human Rights Watch workers interviewed many of the wounded in a hospital in Quetta, Pakistan, and claimed that from 25 to 35 people died in the attack. Foreign media reports, based on more exhaustive interviews, claimed that as many as 93 died.[27] All witnesses denied the existence of any Taliban or al-Qaeda targets in the vicinity, Human Rights Watch reported, adding, "In almost all other cases . . . survivors and witnesses have been forthcoming in identifying Taliban or Al-Qaeda military positions located nearby which could have been the target of the attack."[28] The response of "unidentified Pentagon officials"? Chowkar-Karez was "a fully legitimate target" because the people were Taliban and al-Qaeda sympathizers. "The people there are dead because we wanted them dead," an official said.[29]

Similar targets included a bus traveling north of Kabul, killing 35, a 100-bed military hospital in Herat, a Red Cross dispensary in Kandahar, killing 10, and the aforementioned Red Cross warehouses.

A few days into the bombing, the United States began dropping cluster bombs. A CBU-87 cluster bomb, known as a "combined effects munitions" because it combines anti-personnel, anti-tank, and incendiary capabilities, contains 202 submunitions, or "bomblets," which are typically dispersed over roughly a 50-meter by 100-meter area (a little over one football field — some cluster bombs disperse bomblets over an area the size of several football fields). The bomblets explode near the ground, saturating an area with explosives and tiny shards of steel flying at extremely high velocities. Though they can penetrate light armor, the shards are most effective, by design, against soft targets like people.

By their nature, cluster bombs are extremely difficult to target precisely, thus increasing the likelihood that they will cause disproportionate civilian casualties (according to the laws of war, civilian casualties are allowed as "collateral damage" as long as they are "proportional" to the military objective being achieved). Further complicating the matter, roughly 7 percent (in the CBU-87) of the bomblets fail to explode on impact (this number can rise to 30 percent on soft terrain).

When this happens, the bomblets function as super landmines, waiting for an innocent to come along and touch them, at which point they explode, potentially killing people as far as 50 meters away. The Gulf War, in which there was the greatest use of cluster bombs in history, left 1.2 million unexploded bomblets on the sands of Iraq and Kuwait. Since then, over 1600 Iraqi and Kuwaiti civilians have been killed, and 2500 injured, by them.[30] Unexploded bomblets left in Kosovo killed over 50 people in the year following the war.

Cluster bombs are not covered by the 1997 Mine Ban Treaty, which has 142 signatories (the United States is not one of them), but are essentially equivalent to landmines in their indiscriminate effects, differing only in that an individual bomblet is far more dangerous than a typical landmine. Because of the indiscriminate nature of cluster bombs, both during and after fighting, Human Rights Watch and other groups have called for them to be banned from use.

As of December 6, at least 600 CBU-87 cluster bombs had been dropped on Afghanistan. Assuming a 7 percent failure rate, roughly 8500 unexploded bomblets lay littered across the country.[31] There are numerous reports of civilians being killed by cluster bombs, both by bomblets that exploded on impact and by ones that didn't, including nine dead in the village of Shakar Qala.

On top of that, the cluster bomblets used by the United States are a bright yellow, very similar in color to the much-ballyhooed food packets that were being dropped. Bad enough because bright colors are particularly attractive to children, this multiplied the problem significantly, since Afghans had been repeatedly told to look for the bright yellow packets if they needed food or medicine. When this was pointed out, the United States was forced to interrupt its propaganda broadcasts to say, in Dari and Pashto (the two most common languages in Afghanistan), "Attention, people of Afghanistan! As you may have heard, the Partnership of Nations is dropping yellow Humanitarian Daily Rations. The rations are square-shaped and are packaged in plastic. They are full of good nutritious, Halal food. In areas far from where we are dropping food, we are dropping cluster bombs. Although it is unlikely, it is possible that not every bomb will explode on impact. These bombs are a yellow color and are can-shaped . . . " There are reports of people dying because of mistaking a bomblet for a food packet, to add to those dead because food packets fell in minefields.

On October 31, the Pentagon announced that B-52s were carpet-bombing troop concentrations — although they preferred to say they were dropping "long sticks" of bombs. This technique, carried out against troops utterly unable to defend themselves, killed hundreds or thousands in Serbia, and tens of thousands in Iraq.

Early in November, the Pentagon acknowledged that it had dropped two "daisy cutter" bombs on Taliban positions. The BLU-82, called a "daisy cutter" because of the blast pattern it leaves, is a 15,000-pound bomb so large that it can only be delivered by dropping it out the doors of a cargo plane. The bomb disperses a slurry of ammonium nitrate, aluminum powder, and polystyrene, which it then explosively ignites, causing pressures of over 1000 psi (one atmosphere is 14.7 psi) at the blast center, creating temperatures of over 5000 C, and killing everything within a 300–900 foot radius.[32] Used in Vietnam to clear forest for use as helicopter landing pads, 11 "daisy cutters" were also dropped during the Gulf War. It is the largest non-nuclear bomb in the U.S. arsenal. Given the magnitude of the blast radius, it is necessarily an indiscriminate weapon.

From the first days of the bombing, there were numerous reports of power blackouts in Kabul and Kandahar. Targeting of fuel depots, designed to make military transport more difficult, necessarily made transport of humanitarian supplies more difficult. In fact, there was systematic targeting of what little functioning civilian infrastructure the country had. According to a report by Prof. Marc Herold of the University of New Hampshire,

> On October 15th, U.S bombs destroyed Kabul's main telephone exchange, killing 12. In late October, U.S warplanes bombed the electrical grid in Kandahar knocking out all power, but the Talian were able to divert some electricity to the city from a generating plant in another province, Helmand, but that generation plant [at Kajaki dam] was then bombed. On October 31st, it launched seven air strikes against Afghanistan's largest hydroelectric power station adjacent to the huge Kajaki dam, 90 kilometers northwest of Kandahar, raising fears about the dam breaking.[33]

That damage to the Kajaki complex knocked out power for Kandahar and Lashkarga and faced thousands with the risk of flooding. Inaugurated in 1953, the Kajaki dam on the Helmand River generates 150MW of electric power and irrigates land farmed by 75,000 families. In 2001, Afghanistan was suffering its third year of severe drought, and any threat to water supplies is a serious threat to life.

After the Taliban withdrawal, the bombing around Kandahar and east toward Jalalabad increased in ferocity. On December 1 and 2, strikes near the massive, fortified Tora Bora complex, where according to some reports, bin Laden might have been in hiding, devastated three villages, killing over 100 civilians—some reports claim as many as 300.[34]

Although neither the U.S. government nor the U.S. mass media have attempted publicly to tally the civilian deaths, Herold's exhaustive study, quoted from earlier, estimated that as of December 6, 3,767 civilians had been killed. Although the number is so far beyond the impression given in the U.S. media that it might seem ridiculous, he arrived at the number by exhaustive day-to-day cross-checking of reports from the foreign press, never accepting any report unless it was corroborated by another newspaper, and often not including events where people died but the number had not been determined, and generally taking the lower number if tallies conflicted—so, if anything, the number is more likely to be an underestimate than an overestimate. In January, Herold updated the figure to 4,050—one of the significant additions was the bombing of Qalaye Niazi, a village with no military targets, in which over 100 civilians were killed. Later, in the wake of claims by Afghan newsmen that early in the bombing they were ordered by Taliban authorities to inflate claims of civilian dead, Herold revised his figure to "3000 to 3600."

Although the Pentagon has seriously resisted acknowledging any particular number, even for single incidents, it generally explains away reports of civilian casualties, if they cannot be attributed to inaccuracy or human error, as owing to a Taliban policy of moving "human shields" into military targets. The same accusations were made after the bombing of the Ameriyyah bomb shelter during the Gulf War, which killed between 400 and 1500 women and children. It's an odd claim to make, because, of course, a policy of using "human shields" only works against an enemy with the humanity to refrain from attacking a target that may have large numbers of civilians in it—and that is clearly no more the case here than it was with Ameriyyah.

There is no doubt there have been at least some cases of (futile) attempts to use human shields, but nothing that can account for thousands of dead.

Herold suggests a different explanation — "The explanation is the apparent willingness of U.S military strategists to fire missiles into and drop bombs upon, heavily populated areas of Afghanistan." He goes on to explain, "A legacy of the ten years of civil war during the 80s is that many military garrisons and facilities are located in urban areas where the Soviet-backed government had placed them since they could be better protected there from attacks by the rural mujahideen. Successor Afghan governments inherited these emplacements."

In fact, he says, "When faced with the indisputable 'fact' of having hit a civilian area, the Bush-Blair team responds that a military facility close-by was the target. In every case we can document, this turns out to be a long abandoned military facility." Presumably this indicates a willingness of the Pentagon to risk the lives of Afghan civilians without even bothering to update their intelligence information to see if there are targets worth hitting.

Perhaps partly in response to Herold's report, organizations like Human Rights Watch and the Project for Defense Alternatives (a nonprofit military policy think-tank) did their own studies of the bombing. The PDA's, issued on January 18, 2002, estimated the total number of civilian deaths at 1,000 to 1,300. Even with this lower figure, it concluded that the number of civilians killed per bomb in Afghanistan was about four times that killed in the war on Serbia, even though the proportion of "precision" weapons was twice as high in Afghanistan. The report identified several reasons for this, among them that the precision weapons used in Afghanistan were much more likely to be GPS-directed (Global Positioning System) rather than laser-guided (GPS bombs are less precise, and often termed "near-precision" weapons), increased percentages of cluster bombs (10–15 percent as opposed to 7 percent in Serbia), increased use of bombers rather than fighters (and among them increased reliance on the older B-52s), and more relaxed rules for acquiring "targets of opportunity" because of the relative paucity of predetermined, fixed targets as compared with the case of Serbia. Except for noting that another difference was an explicit policy of "regime change" in Afghanistan, and the desire to hunt down al-Qaeda members, the report did not speculate on underlying reasons for these differences. It is not hard to guess that among the reasons may well have been the diminished effect on the American public of viewing non-white Afghan "collateral damage" as opposed to white Serbian victims, as well as the fact that Serbian victims and friends and relations of victims could report what happened to the world over the Internet, unlike Afghans, who were totally dependent on Western media coverage of their plight.

Although this newer report, with its lower number of victims and its seemingly greater institutional authority, has generally been represented as far more reliable than Herold's report, it is worth noting several severe limitations in its methodology that the Herold report does not share. To begin with, Herold's report considers the mainstream press of any country (outside Afghanistan) to be a legitimate source, while the PDA's report openly enshrines the implicit notion of cultural supremacy so much relied on by the Pentagon, treating anything that is not corroborated by a report in the "Western" media as "unconfirmed" and dismissing it. The report also notes that survivors' accounts of the number of victims often differ significantly from the conclusions of Western journalists on the scene, but for some unexplained reason ignores the systematic biases that would tend to make journalists' figures lower (such as only reporting verifiable and corroborated claims), and assumes that journalists' figures are the correct ones. In a particularly stunning account of its biased methodology, the report admits, "For the purposes of the present study, when Afghan refugee or government reports were expressed in vague terms, the following reduction factors were used to derive an estimate: 'some or a few' deaths was interpreted as 1, 'a dozen or more' was interpreted as 3–4, 'dozens' was interpreted as 8–10, 'scores' was interpreted as 10–15, 'hundreds' was interpreted as 40–60." Although such a methodology might serve well in determining a lower bound on casualties, to assign an upper bound when there is such systematic reduction of reported figures is insupportable, and, frankly, unconscionable.

The casualty figures, whichever you choose to believe, emphasize one of the fundamental problems with modern U.S. aerial bombing campaigns. The desire to minimize the risk to U.S. soldiers, no matter what the cost to civilians, means that planes fly very high, making it virtually certain that there will be frequent misidentification of targets and decreasing the accuracy of bombing. In order to obey the laws of war, and to make sure there are not disproportionate effects on civilians, it is necessary for each side to subject its soldiers to some risk. Indeed, these results pose once again the question of whether aerial bombing campaigns in and of themselves necessarily have a disproportionate effect on civilians. Morally, of course, the distinction between "intent" to kill civilians and deliberately embarking on a course of action that will almost certainly kill civilians is negligible.

In addition to all the deaths mentioned above are the deaths caused by creation of hundreds of thousands and perhaps over 1 million refugees and severe disruption of aid programs, which will likely kill far more than were actually blown apart, shot, or incinerated directly. While it is impossible to calculate, it's hard to imagine, given that 100 per day were dying in one refugee camp, that the total number is less than tens of thousands — and the results are not yet in on whether the spring harvest will fail due to disruption of the fall planting by bombing, possibly ushering in famine once again. The number of Taliban and al-Qaeda fighters killed may never be tallied, but is unlikely to be small, given the horrifically destructive nature of the weapons used against them.

9. A War for Civilization

Any lingering feelings that this was, as it was constantly touted to be, a war of civilization against barbarism should have been dispelled by late November. After the Taliban's precipitous withdrawal, within a space of days, from 80 percent of Afghanistan, it soon turned out that there was a considerable residual force of Taliban fighters cut off at Kunduz, a city in the north. Variously estimated at up to 20,000 soldiers, it included perhaps several thousand foreigners — most of them Arabs, Chechens, and Pakistanis, but also some Chinese, Indonesians, Filipinos, and even a few white Americans. Besieged by Northern Alliance forces and continually pounded by U.S. bombing, the fighters had no hope of prevailing. In order to avert needless bloodshed, Northern Alliance commanders met with commanders from the other side to work out surrender terms. Those negotiations were made far more difficult and dangerous by U.S. intervention.

Alarmed by reports that some commanders were considering allowing safe passage for fighters who laid down their arms, Rumsfeld said America was "not inclined to negotiate surrenders," indicating that he was concerned that no Taliban be allowed to escape, even unarmed. Later, he "clarified" the statement — Afghan Taliban could be allowed out, but, for foreign fighters, "My hope is that they will either be killed or taken prisoner."[35] It did not appear to matter which; he added, "Any idea that those people should end up in some sort of a negotiation which would allow them to leave the country and go off and destabilize other countries and engage in terrorist attacks on the U.S. is something that I would certainly do everything I could to prevent."

It was repeatedly made clear that the United States had no interest in taking them prisoner, because of lack of forces on the ground. Given the history of both the Northern Alliance and the Taliban of massacring prisoners (after the Taliban were driven out of Mazar-i-Sharif in 1997, an estimated 3000 prisoners were killed by the Northern Alliance by being thrown into wells, followed by grenades, being slowly asphyxiated in metal shipping containers, and similar methods), anything less than a strong statement that the laws of war required that prisoners be treated humanely was inexcusable. Instead, Rumsfeld chose essentially to incite the Northern Alliance to massacre.

A 1977 protocol additional to the Geneva Convention makes it illegal "to order that there shall be no survivors." Although Mr. Rumsfeld did not "order" that there be no survivors, the clear import of his words was that survivors were not particularly wanted. British military historian John Keegan, writing in the London *Daily Telegraph*, said of Rumsfeld's call, "Mr. Rumsfeld, in his recent statements, has made it clear that swift, local brutality may cause the problem to disappear. Better not to speculate about the detail. We are dealing with the modern equivalent of pirates and bandits, whose fate was sealed historically by peremptory measures. That may be the best way out."

Shortly after these statements, there were claims that Afghan fighters who wanted to surrender were being forced to continue fighting by the foreigners, who adamantly opposed surrender—hardly a surprising reaction to being told that effectively no quarter would be given.

While many foreigners were eventually taken prisoner without being massacred, there were several disturbing events, including especially a prison uprising in Qala-i-Jangi, a fort near Mazar-i-Sharif where roughly 800 prisoners were being held. Supposedly, the uprising started when two American CIA employees entered a holding cell to interrogate some foreigners. On being asked why they had come to Afghanistan, one replied, "To kill people like you," rushing at them as he answered. One CIA operative, Johnny "Mike" Spann, was taken and beaten to death, while the other shot his way out. Some prisoners then broke free, killing several Northern Alliance guards. According to different versions, some had not been properly disarmed when taken prisoner, or some broke into arms caches in the fort. The uprising was put down by 500-pound bombs dropped from the air and strafing by American helicopter gunships, in addition to tank attacks from the Northern Alliance. After three days, resistance was over, and more than 600 prisoners dead.

Some reports indicated that hundreds of the dead had their hands tied behind their backs. There was no explanation of why there was a need for aerial bombing to put down a prison riot. At the very least, given that so many were incapacitated, the response was extremely disproportionate, and a war crime. Both the United States and Britain announced that they saw no need for an inquiry into the events even though Amnesty International called for an inquiry, and the Northern Alliance agreed to allow it.

After the attacks on the fort were over, 80 prisoners were re-captured, indicating that at least many of the prisoners had no intrinsic desire to fight to the death. Given the oft-repeated American wish to see the "foreign" fighters dead, it's likely the prisoners felt they would be killed anyway, and so had no choice but to rebel. It is certainly clear that the fact that prisoners could get access to weapons was a result either of negligence or of a desire to manufacture an excuse for killing them.

A counterpoint to all of these events was the bizarre debate that had been raging for weeks on American TV screens. "If Osama bin Laden walks toward American forces with his hands up, do we take him prisoner or do we kill him?" The question was most often asked by news anchors in slightly hectoring tones of present or retired military officers. Responses ranged from wooden responses that the Geneva Convention required allowing him to surrender (usually from lower-level officers) to a nod and a wink and a suggestion that we'd all like to see bin Laden dead (from higher officers or government officials).

In fact, in early December, as Afghans fighting against the Taliban and al-Qaeda negotiated with al-Qaeda fighters trapped in Tora Bora for them to surrender, the United States moved in to scuttle the deal. "The Americans won't accept their surrender," Hazrat Ali, regional security chief for eastern Afghanistan, said, after emerging from hours of negotiations with U.S. officials. "They want to kill them."[36] Without judging whether such a perception is fully accurate, the fact that many Afghans have it is undoubtedly significant.

A final uncivilized episode in this war for civilization was the treatment of al-Qaeda prisoners transported to the U.S. base at Guantanamo Bay, Cuba. They were transported shackled hand and foot, with sacks tied over their heads, often sedated. They were kept in open-air cells, exposed to the elements, shaved of hair and beards even though this violated their religious beliefs, forced to sleep with bright arc lights illuminating every inch of their surroundings, and subjected to extensive interrogations. All of these acts, and also the televising of the prisoners, are violations of the Geneva Convention, but the United States government has claimed that the Geneva Convention does not apply to them. The reasoning given is that the Geneva Convention applies to prisoners of war, but these people are terrorists, not soldiers. As we will discuss later, this means that they are not really entitled to a fair trial with full due process of law. These explanations miss the not-so-subtle point that one cannot assume guilt before trial — whatever rights terrorists may have, these men have not yet been proven to be terrorists — and, as anyone else presumed innocent, whether an American citizen or not, have the right to full representation in American courts.

If this war were really being fought for civilization, there would be less desire to contravene some of civilization's most basic principles.

10. A War on Terrorism

Just as what this war was fought for differs from the official story, so does what this war was fought against. While it is certainly being fought against certain terrorists, it is anything but a war on terrorism.

To start with, the bombing of Afghanistan has allowed the Northern Alliance to take over most of the country. By any meaningful definition of terrorism, they are as much terrorists as the Taliban. After they took Kabul in 1992, they dissolved into internecine warfare, with civilian populations caught in the middle. Their indiscriminate artillery attacks killed up to 50,000 civilians in Kabul alone before the Taliban conquered it in 1996. They have committed ethnically based massacres, massacre of prisoners (mentioned earlier), mass rape, forced marriage (i.e. repeated rape), torture, and other crimes. Not only that, they left the countryside so disorganized and prey to bandits and ruffians that many saw the advent of the Taliban as positive because they provided some public order.

Since the Northern Alliance started taking over, allegations of crimes against humanity have been rampant. Taliban prisoners, disarmed and begging for their lives, have been beaten and stabbed to death. Prisoners have been lined up and shot. The Associated Press reported, "Stomping on faces of captured Taliban and shooting others as they lay wounded, opposition forces rampaged through Kunduz on Monday [November 26]." There are allegations that in late November, in the town of Takhteh Pol on the road between Kandahar and Pakistan, Alliance commanders ordered the machine-gunning of 160 Taliban prisoners. This was just one of several similar incidents.

The Revolutionary Association of the Women of Afghanistan, a group of exceptionally brave women who conduct literacy classes, build hospitals, and make secret trips with video cameras to document life under the Taliban—and have been subjected to tremendous media attention and adulation since September 11—had repeatedly called for the United States not to help put the Northern Alliance in power. Those calls went unheeded, as, with only pro forma objections (the U.S. government called on the Alliance not to enter

Kabul), the United States created the conditions that would allow the Alliance to sweep into Kabul and other cities.

The U.S. strategy has involved abetting a number of other kinds of terrorism. Russia has come under severe international opprobrium, including from the United States, for the conduct of its war on Chechnya. Russia treats this problem as one of terrorism, and so has been happy to make common cause with the United States. And, in fact, it has suffered terrorist attacks committed by Islamic fundamentalist Chechen separatists, such as a series of bomb blasts on housing complexes, including one on September 13, 1999, on a Moscow apartment complex, that killed over 100 people. But Russia has also committed high-level state terrorism itself, mercilessly bombing Grozny, the capital of Chechnya, in December 1999. Part of the current U.S.–Russia rapprochement involves the United States keeping silent over Chechnya in return for Russian support for U.S. crimes in Afghanistan.

China has also seen cooperation with the United States as a way to give it a free hand to commit more state terrorism in its war against Islamic fundamentalist Uigur separatists.

Pakistan, the most important U.S. ally in the war on Afghanistan, has long been guilty of financing, training, and inserting into Kashmir armed Islamic fundamentalist terrorists, who have caused the vast majority of the Hindu population of the valley to flee. India, another major ally, has been committing serious state terrorism in Kashmir.

The United States has also not seen fit to turn over any of the terrorists it currently harbors to justice—a list ranging from Emanuel Constant of the Haitian death squads to right-wing anti-Castro Cubans to south Lebanese Phalangist militiamen who killed two Irish peacekeepers to Henry Kissinger. Nor has it seen fit to shut down the terrorist training camp it runs at Fort Benning, Georgia. Formerly known as the School of the Americas, it currently goes by the name Western Hemisphere Institute for Security Cooperation— largely in response to protests designed to shut it down.

The School of the Americas first came into the news in a major way in 1992, with the release of a declassified SOA manual that suggested torture and assassination as useful techniques in dealing with political movements. Over its decades of existence, it has graduated hundreds of future military dictators, death squad leaders, torturers, and others who have spread misery throughout Latin America. Graduates include Roberto D'Aubuisson, who organized the death squad network in El Salvador (right-wing terror claimed roughly 50,000 lives there), and orchestrated the assassination of Archbishop Oscar Romero in 1980; former military dictator of Bolivia Hugo Banzer Suarez; Efraim Rios Montt, whose reign of terror over Guatemala in the early 1980s saw the killing of over 100,000 Mayan Indians; General Roberto Viola, briefly military dictator of Argentina, who has been convicted of murder, kidnapping, and torture during its "dirty war" in the 1970s; and many more. Although incriminating references like those in the old manual have been excised, and it is now claimed that "human rights" training is a major part of the curriculum, there is little doubt that it exists for the same purpose it always has, with the same kinds of instructors teaching the same kinds of pupils.

Nor has it seen fit to withdraw its support for Israeli state terrorism against the Palestinians in the occupied territories, which regularly involves attacks with advanced military equipment against the populace. Proclaimed as attacks on militants, they frequently kill innocent bystanders, children, pregnant women, and others who have not been involved in violent acts. On the contrary, not long after declaration of the war on terrorism, Congress voted its annual appropriation of military and "economic development" aid (the latter is effectively military aid, because it frees up funds that are generally used to buy U.S. weapons)—this year, it was $2.76 billion.

11. Fighting for Our Security

Even more doubtful was the claim that the policies being undertaken were designed to safeguard the security of the American public. Instead, the pattern seen over and over was an opportunistic invocation of security to sell policies that sometimes had nothing to do with security and sometimes clearly increased risks to security.

Perhaps the most obvious was the bombing of Afghanistan. This was widely understood to be an act that would increase the threat of terrorist attacks in the future. The anger it has generated in the Islamic world is tremendous, far greater even than that generated by the Gulf War. Millions of Afghans have turned against the United States as more and more civilians were killed and forced to become refugees by the bombing—and Afghanistan was notable for its almost complete lack of anti-American sentiment before the bombing.

The bombing has occasioned numerous protests across the Islamic world. Protests staged by Islamic fundamentalists in Pakistan were put down by force, with several people killed. Protests in the occupied territories met a similar fate, repressed by the Palestinian Authority with at least two killed. Although nowhere have the protests reached the point of destabilizing governments, that is testimony to the extremely efficient and brutal methods of repression used against them and to the fact that bin Laden and his ilk, unlike genuine freedom fighters, have such a very unappealing agenda, with little to offer most people. It is notable that bin Laden has become a hero to many in the Islamic world, not because they approve of the September 11 attack but because they see him standing up to U.S. aggression.

The fact that the bombing did not occasion an immediate counterattack is no cause for complacency. It has laid the foundation for future terrorist attacks, which will be years and decades in the making, not weeks or months. It has been a far more effective recruiting vehicle than anything bin Laden could have done. There is a tendency to dismiss such warnings as crying wolf; however, similar warnings after the Gulf War were also dismissed as alarmist, a conclusion many might wish to revisit after the events of September 11. The requirements of empire are very different from, and often at odds with, considerations of safety.

In a similar vein were the calls to "free the CIA" to do its supposed job of ferreting out information about threats to the United States. Retired government officials and media pundits made the rounds, telling us that the CIA had been "emasculated," hemmed in by bureaucracy and concern about human rights. The 1975 Church Commission, one of the few truly laudable congressional initiatives in foreign policy, which exposed a whole array of brutal and illegal actions by the nation's intelligence apparatus (including *inter alia* the assassination of Patrice Lumumba of Zaire, seven attempts to assassinate Fidel Castro of Cuba, involvement in the 1965 military coup in Indonesia that led to the massacre of 500,000–1,000,000 alleged Communists), came in for a special share of opprobrium. Others chose the "human rights" presidency of Jimmy Carter for disdain.

Others focused on a 1995 change in CIA rules, promulgated in response to revelations that CIA agents had been involved in killing an American citizen in Guatemala, that required that CIA operatives in the field get permission from headquarters before working with anyone with a criminal background or a record of violating human rights. Many mistakenly claimed that it was an absolute prohibition on working with criminals, rather than a mere requirement to check in.

The common refrain was that you can't find out what terrorists are doing without dealing with terrorists, so the rules make no sense. The implication was that concern with human rights was at best an impossible luxury, at worst criminal stupidity. The truth is that the CIA does things, competently or not, much as it always did. Whatever the restrictions brought upon it by the Church Commission and the Carter administration it was still able after all of that to carry out its biggest operation ever, the Afghan jihad in the 1980s. The supposed concern over human rights did not stop them from training and financing the contras, an army of thugs turned loose to attack "soft targets" in Nicaragua (i.e., unarmed peasants), unleashing torture, rape, and murder across the land—not to mention funding their activities by smuggling cocaine to street dealers across the United States to be sold as crack.[37]

The 1995 rule change was more cosmetic than real. CIA spokesman Bill Harlow, appearing on CNN News on October 6, was quick to deny the pundits' claims, saying, "We have continued to deal with people with unsavory backgrounds, because we know better than anyone else that that's who you need to deal with in order to get the information you need on terrorism," adding, "we have never turned down an opportunity to recruit a terrorist because of a human rights background." According to the *Christian Science Monitor*, "Insiders say the top brass seldom rejects a request."[38]

The main issue, however, is that the CIA has had a large part in creating the problem in the first place. Many analysts have pointed out how the Taliban and Osama bin Laden are what is termed "blowback" in the intelligence community—in other words they are "side effects" of previous CIA operations. The CIA-sponsored Afghan war helped create, train, and arm the groups of militants that were involved in the attacks of September 11. CIA coups have helped keep the Islamic world festering under corrupt dictatorial regimes, thus dramatically increasing the pool from which terrorist organizations draw recruits. CIA operations have helped create resentment of the United States all around the world.

If anything should be on the table with regard to the CIA, it should be restricting, not expanding, its operations. Recruiting groups of thugs and then training them in sophisticated military tactics, giving them money and arms, creates very dangerous groups of thugs. Even in the abstract, that would seem to increase the risks to security of people everywhere, including in the United States. Concretely, New York City is dealing with the effects of that right now.

In general, the response to the attacks has been to continue and intensify failed policies. U.S. military aggression, covert operations, and generally throwing its weight around as the only superpower have led straight to the attacks of September 11 (of course, to talk about their causes is not in any way to justify the attacks, any more than talk about the causes of ordinary crime is a justification of it). Albert Einstein once defined insanity as doing the same thing again and again, expecting different results.

The Bush administration again showed its lack of concern for genuine security issues, and its inclination to opportunistic exploitation of security concerns, when one of its first reactions to the attacks was to call for swift passage of an appropriation for their much-debated National Missile Defense program. In a short time, $8.3 billion (for the 2002 budget) was voted, without demurral, for a program that was set to be very hotly debated had the attacks not occurred.

Of course, even a missile defense system like Reagan's initial pie-in-the-sky Star Wars idea (not even remotely feasible with today's technology) would have been useless against the attacks that actually occurred. Worse than that, Missile Defense is not really defensive at all — any state intent on successfully launching ballistic missiles at the United States (only China, Russia, France, and the United Kingdom can do it now) could easily fool any such system with decoys. If anything, it increases risks to security by encouraging proliferation of nuclear weapons, especially by China. Missile Defense is projected to cost at least $60 billion, on top of the $70 billion spent so far — some projections run to $120 billion.

Similarly useless was the October 26 awarding of a contract to Lockheed Martin for the long-proposed joint-strike fighter. Potentially the largest contract in Department of Defense history, it may cost as much as $200 billion — twice that if one includes potential foreign sales. This at a time when U.S. military technology is already a decade ahead of its close allies and several ahead of any potential foes. Just like Missile Defense, the joint-strike fighter is about proliferation, not security — sell enough state-of-the-art planes to other countries, then you can argue that you need a new generation of planes. Once that new generation is created, it's all the easier to sell older planes.

Equally remarkable was the Bush administration's plan to "fight terrorism" by ending all congressional restrictions on arms sales. Currently, the law prohibits sales of arms to states that violate human rights or for purposes that violate international law. Although the law is regularly violated with regard to favored client states like Israel and Turkey, it has at times been used to limit Washington's support for repressive regimes. Most notable, perhaps, is the great success by thousands of dedicated activists in the East Timor Action Network to get Congress to end arms sales to Indonesia, which invaded East Timor in 1975, conducting a genocidal military campaign and establishing a military occupation that lasted until 1999. The idea behind the proposal was to allow sales to countries like Syria, if they cooperated in the war against ter-

rorism. Not only have U.S. arms sales caused the deaths of countless numbers, they have been of particular importance in keeping the dictatorial
regimes of the Arab world in power, thus increasing the pool of potential terrorists. They are also frequently used against U.S. forces. Congressional opposition forced the administration to shelve that idea.

There are other examples of the government holding free market dogma
above security concerns. With airport security on everyone's agenda, and with
a renewed appreciation for the public sector, the Senate unanimously passed
a bill to nationalize airport security. Ever since airline deregulation in 1978,
airport security has been up to the airlines, which outsource it to private security firms. To maximize profits, these firms cut labor costs to the bone—as well
as overhead like background checks and legal oversight.

Argenbright, the largest security firm, has been convicted of hiring numerous felons through deliberately avoiding background checks and forging documents to cover up that fact. In lieu of the 40-hour training they're supposed
to provide, they often simply show new employees a 45-minute video and put
them to work. They've hired hundreds of employees who have either failed a
test required by the FAA or never taken it at all. Since September 11, there
have been numerous instances of passengers taking knives and even guns
through Argenbright checkpoints. Employees are paid barely more than minimum wage, and generally get no health or other benefits. On September 15th,
the *San Francisco Chronicle* reported that according to the latest report of the
U.S. General Accounting Office, the investigative arm of Congress, the
turnover averaged 126 percent at the 19 large U.S. airports that were surveyed.
At Boston's Logan International, where two of the hijacked planes took off, the
entire staff was replaced twice during the 11-month survey period—hardly a
way to ensure consistent performance.

Airport security, like health-care, is an area where the shortcomings of
"free enterprise" are particularly obvious—a largely captive market means
there is very little dependence of demand on the quality of service, so the
incentive to maximize profits by cutting costs reigns supreme. In practice,
this means providing the least service with the least care, and paying people
as little as possible—which is not much of an incentive to be vigilant. The
difference between police and private rent-a-cops is suggestive of the difference between current airport security personnel and government employees
in a nationalized system.

Nonetheless, the Bush administration vowed to oppose the Senate plan, aided by some House Republicans — heavy lobbying and phone-calling from the White House led to defeat of the plan in the House by a vote of 218–214. In the end, the bill on airport security was only passed on November 20, with the result that the government was unable even to consider implementing it before January 2002. On November 17th, Transportation Secretary Norman Mineta said that the government would not meet a January deadline for screening all checked airline baggage — one of the key provisions of the aviation security bill.

The anthrax scare was another front on which the administration quickly dropped any pretense of pressing concern for the real security and well-being of the American people at the first sign of risk to corporate profitability. As several letters tainted with anthrax spores were sent to a variety of media and congressional targets, resulting in the death of five people, the government made plans to stockpile Cipro, the only antibiotic approved by the FDA for treating anthrax. Bayer holds the patent for the drug, and, as is normal in the industry, charges prices practically unrelated to the cost of production.

Even though Bayer was unable to produce the required number of pills before January 2002, the government decided early on not to license any other corporations to make the medicine. Bayer initially asked $1.77 per pill, which the government negotiated down to 95 cents per pill — the Indian company Cipla had offered to provide it at 10 cents per pill, but the government refused, too intent on preserving the sanctity of intellectual property rights.

Compulsory licensing (compulsory in the sense that the patent holder has no choice about it, although it still gets royalties) of pharmaceuticals in a potential health emergency is common practice, allowed both by the laws of this country and by international trade laws. The U.S. government regularly issues compulsory licenses for a wide variety of goods produced by foreign corporations. Bayer is a foreign corporation, so one might have thought there would be no problem in this case. Unfortunately, the latest round of WTO negotiations, in Doha, Qatar, were coming up and intellectual property rights in the pharmaceutical arena were going to be a major topic of contention, so the United States didn't want to undercut its position by appearing hypocritical, trying to keep poor countries from licensing production of AIDS drugs while licensing Cipro itself. Also, the company that stood to benefit if the government went with the lowest bidder was an Indian company, not an American one. The consideration of getting enough antibiotics to protect its citizens against a possible anthrax epidemic was apparently not in the picture.

12. United We Stand

As people around the country came together, spontaneously offering help and sharing suffering, waving flags not just out of jingoism or patriotism but also because of a desire to show solidarity and belong to a community, a certain motto kept cropping up on billboards, in TV commercials, and everywhere one turned—"United We Stand."

It was a nice thought. The attacks were terrible, but at least we were coming together as a nation. Unfortunately, it was quickly seized on by opportunists of various stripes. A whole slew of corporations used that motto, images of the flag, and tributes to the New York firefighters in an attempt to suggest that true patriotism involved buying their products. General Motors' ads asking people to buy GM trucks to "keep America rolling" were rather offensive, but pretty typical of the breed.

Numerous politicians and media pundits used it to suggest that standing united meant "uniting behind the president," which in turn meant uncritically supporting everything he called for. Congress took the idea so far that it passed, by a vote of 420–1 in the House and 98–0 in the Senate, a resolution stating that "the president is authorized to use all necessary and appropriate force against those nations, organizations, or persons he determines planned, authorized, committed, or aided the terrorist attacks that occurred on September 11, 2001, or harbored such organizations or persons." Not only did it completely abdicate its authority, as defined in the Constitution, to make decisions about war and peace, it did so for an indefinite period against unspecified enemies—one man could decide to use force against anyone he chose, in any manner he chose, as long as he deemed it "necessary and appropriate." Only Democratic Representative Barbara Lee of California marred that perfect political lockstep.

The fact that the notion of turning over all power to one man, whether elected or not, is deeply antithetical to any notion of democracy, and has nothing to do with the basic human solidarity implied (albeit with generally more than a touch of jingoism and nationalism) by "United We Stand" did not deter government officials in the slightest.

Within weeks of the attack, U.S. Trade Rep. Robert Zoellick decided to link the upcoming vote on "Trade Promotion Authority," commonly known as "Fast Track," to the war on terrorism, declaring that trade "promotes the values at the heart of this protracted struggle." Fast Track authority would give the president the power to present the entire draft of any trade agree-

ment, in particular the Free Trade Area of the Americas agreement (currently being negotiated by 34 countries in the Western Hemisphere), to Congress
to be voted up or down, with no amendments and minimal discussion possible. In his speech to the House on the day it passed by a narrow partisan vote
of 215–214, Speaker Dennis Hastert said, "This Congress will either support
our president, who's fighting a courageous war on terrorism and redefining
American world leadership, or it will undercut the president at the worst possible time."[39]

In a similar vein, Attorney General John Ashcroft, when speaking before
the Senate Judiciary Committee about the Justice Department's investigation,
which has involved serious violation of civil and human rights (to be covered
later), said, "To those . . . who scare peace-loving people with phantoms of lost
liberty, my message is this: Your tactics only aid terrorists, for they erode our
national unity and diminish our resolve."

And yet those who so cavalierly threw around the idea of unity to serve the
prerogatives of power, had a very different idea of the concept when it came to
providing for the ordinary people victimized by the events of September 11 and
their aftermath. That concept came through most clearly in the treatment of
the airline industry by Congress. That industry, already in a fragile state before
September 11 due to the recession, was the most immediately and directly
affected by the attacks; first by the FAA grounding of all planes and then by the
tremendous reduction in travel volume. Shortly after the attacks, several airlines announced massive layoffs, totaling roughly 140,000 workers. They also
took the opportunity to claim, because of exigent circumstances, that they had
no obligation to provide severance pay or transitional health benefits. Though
some airlines, like American, caved in to pressure from unions and did actually award severance pay, there was no question that many of the laid-off airline
employees were in a very difficult position.

Within less than two weeks, both houses had passed a bill providing a $15
billion bailout, some in cash and some in loan guarantees, for the airline
industry—i.e., the executives and stockholders. Congress did not make that
aid conditional on retaining the laid-off workers or even on providing them
any protection. Three months after the attacks, no compensation is yet forthcoming for the workers.

The "economic stimulus package," which passed by the House by a narrowly partisan vote of 216–214 (but didn't pass the Senate), was another case in
point. Although Rep. Bill Thomas of California, the main author of the
Republican plan, made an emotional evocation of "the hardware store, the

diner down the street, the gas station on the corner," the truth is that the lion's share of the over $100 billion in tax cuts would go to large corporations.

Perhaps the most objectionable point, a clear example of corporations feeding at the public trough, was a proposed repeal of the corporate alternative minimum tax (passed in 1986 to reduce corporate abuse of tax loopholes), not just for the current year, but retroactive through 1986. This would have given $25.4 billion in rebates to corporations, with $2.4 billion going to Ford, $1.4 billion to IBM, $572 million to ChevronTexaco, and $254 million to the now-bankrupt Enron, the corporation most closely associated with George W. Bush. Since there were no strings attached to the rebates, even mainstream economists could not see how any of these rebates would stimulate the economy—as Paul Krugman wrote in the *New York Times* (October 28), "a potential investment that Texas Utilities or ChevronTexaco wouldn't have made a week ago, because the project won't yield a sufficiently high return, will seem no more profitable after each company gets its $600 million thank-you gift."

The attitude of the powerful to national unity may have been best summed up by the response to the various anthrax letters. The response to the letter sent to Senate Democratic leader Tom Daschle was immediate, with elaborate quarantine procedures and testing for anthrax set up immediately. By contrast, when authorities found out which postal center the letter had gone through, they did nothing for over three days. Similarly, the letter sent to Tom Brokaw of NBC occasioned an immediate response with regard to the NBC offices. Two days after authorities learned that the letter had gone through Trenton, they said there were no plans to test employees there. On October 21, Thomas L. Morris called 911 and told the operator that he had been exposed to powder in an envelope in the postal facility where he worked and he thought he had anthrax. He died from anthrax a few hours later, as did another postal worker at the same facility, Joseph P. Curseen, Jr. Morris had even seen a doctor, to whom he mentioned his suspicion that he had anthrax. He was sent home with Tylenol. Both were African-American.

The excuse generally given for the delay in helping the postal employees is that even health experts had no idea that someone could be infected through a sealed letter. The fact that that is more of a rationalization than a reason is pointed up by an even more remarkable disparity—legislative aides and political workers on Capitol Hill were given a 60-day supply of Cipro, while postal workers were given a 10-day supply.[40]

13. Restricting Freedom in Defense of Freedom

"Liberties Curtailed in Defense of Freedom" was the title of the lead article in the October 11, 2001, issue of the satirical magazine *The Onion*. The article quoted Attorney General John Ashcroft as supposedly saying "Now is not the time to allow simplistic, romantic notions of 'civil liberties' and 'equal protection under the law' to get in the way of our battle with the enemies of freedom." Although the satire was hardly subtle, the picture painted was not far from the truth.

The administration keeps claiming that the September 11 attacks were an attack on freedom. However, the real attack on freedom came from the Bush administration, with Ashcroft leading the charge. In the aftermath of the attacks, it was clear that people were going to have to give up a few of the privileges they took for granted, like the ability to get to the airport 20 minutes before your flight and still make it onto the plane. Unfortunately, in the main recurring theme of the "war on terrorism," the administration opportunistically took advantage of the situation to ram through an agenda based more on control and power than on security — in this case, legislation abrogating fundamental civil liberties. Most of the provisions proposed by the administration are at best of dubious use in catching prospective terrorists, but will likely prove useful in curtailing domestic political action and protest and increasing government's power to enforce the status quo. These steps have also continued the disturbing but long-standing process of transferring power in criminal matters from the judicial to the executive branch.

The "Uniting and Strengthening America by Providing Appropriate Tools Required to Intercept and Obstruct Terrorism," or USA PATRIOT Act, was signed into law on October 26. It had passed the Senate with only one dissenting vote, Russell Feingold of Wisconsin, and with minimal dissent in the House.

It provides for "roving" wiretaps — previously, a wiretap order had to specify a particular phone, but now a single order can cover any phone the mentioned person is likely to use. On the surface, this might not seem problematic, but such an order covers a person's work phone and even pay phones near the person's house, devices that may be used by large numbers of people with no reason to suppose their words are being recorded.

It allows for a great expansion of searches without notification to the target, either before or after. Such "no-tell" searches were previously very rare, but now can be done with regard to any criminal investigation whatsoever.

It allows dramatically expanded sharing of information between law-enforcement and intelligence agencies, including the release of previously protected grand jury information; according to the American Civil Liberties Union, this has "effectively put the CIA back in the business of spying on Americans." This had been common practice in the 60s and early 70s—under Operation CHAOS, the CIA collected information on over 7000 Americans, anti-Vietnam-war activists, student activists, black nationalists, and other opponents of the established order. Once information sharing was allowed, the CIA had merely to express a request for certain types of information, and domestic law enforcement agencies would find it. The Church Committee, in its report on intelligence activities, concluded, "To the extent that [the] information related to domestic activity, its maintenance by the CIA, although perhaps not itself the performance of an internal security function, is a step toward the dangers of a domestic secret police."[41]

It also provides intelligence agencies access to a broad array of information from school records, financial transactions, and Internet activity. Simultaneously, the standard of evidence required for obtaining a court order for any of the above activities has been greatly weakened—now, all law enforcement agencies need to claim is that the information is "relevant" to an investigation.

Another very troubling aspect of the USA PATRIOT Act is the creation of a new category of crime, "domestic terrorism." The term is so broadly defined that it includes use of a "firearm, weapon or other dangerous device . . . to cause substantial damage to property," if it's for a political cause. The phrase "weapon or other dangerous device" was added to a previous clause defining terrorism so that the new law can potentially cover acts like throwing a rock through a window. It is hard to interpret this provision except as a way to define political protest, like some of the actions in "anti-corporate-globalization" protests like the one at Seattle or like many actions undertaken by environmentalists and animal rights activists, as terrorism. This comes on top of a dramatic reinterpretation of existing law that has involved preventive detention, mass arrests of people congregated on a sidewalk (in Washington, D.C., at the IMF/World Bank protest on April 16, 2000), brutal police assaults on peaceful protesters, and the imposition of up to $1 million in bail for people accused of a minor civil offense because they looked like organizers (during the Philadelphia protests at the Republican National Convention).

Worst of all, the USA PATRIOT Act dramatically extends the deprivation of basic rights of immigrants begun with the 1996 "Antiterrorism and Effective Death Penalty Act," passed largely in response to the Oklahoma City bombing, which, of course, involved no immigrants. That act involved measures like the use of secret evidence against immigrants in deportation hearings, a severe violation of the fundamental right of due process. The abuses involved were so severe that the Clinton administration had largely stopped using secret evidence and Bush had promised not to use it either—since September 11, however, secret evidence is once again in use.

In addition, the new law extends from 48 hours to 7 days the period non-citizens can be held without being charged with a crime—the administration had originally pushed to be able to hold them indefinitely. In fact, if said person cannot be deported for some reason, he or she can be held indefinitely—and, of course, few countries will take back someone accused by the United States government of being a terrorist. Such detention requires only the attorney general's certification that there are "reasonable grounds to believe" the non-citizen endangers national security.

The law also provides that non-citizens can be detained or deported for giving money to any organization that may be, under the broad definition used previously, involved in terrorism. This comes on top of years of prosecution of people for giving money to hospitals and community welfare programs run by groups with an illegal wing. This action can be taken even if the group involved is not on the government's list of terrorist organizations. The burden of proof is on the non-citizen to show that the assistance rendered was not intended to aid or abet terrorism—the detainee is required to prove a negative.

The dragnet put out by the Justice Department since September 11 has already been responsible for numerous abuses of the rights of non-citizens. Over 1200 people had been taken into custody as of this writing, and nearly half, an estimated 550, were still in custody, some of them since just days after the attacks. Many have been held incommunicado, with not even their families notified of their whereabouts. Many have been repeatedly denied access to their lawyers. One person has already died in custody, from a heart attack. Another, a Pakistani youth, was stripped and beaten by his cell-mates, who repeatedly addressed him as "bin Laden," while guards looked on.

Until late November, the Justice Department had released no information on detainees. Even when it did, the information was dramatically insufficient. On December 5, a group of 16 human rights and civil liberties organizations filed suit to obtain basic information, including "the identity of the detainees, where they are being held, the names of their lawyers, which courts are involved, how long the detainees have been held and the nature of any charges filed against them."[42]

According to various news reports, only 27 of these people are thought to have some information regarding the attacks. Most others are being held for minor immigration infractions. Many have been held for months without being charged, in violation even of the USA PATRIOT Act's provisions, let alone of those in force when they were detained. Equally amazing, the attorney general has been authorized to record conversations between detainees and their lawyers, without even a need for a court order. This violates attorney-client privilege, universally recognized as integral to a defendant's ability to mount the best possible defense and thus to due process.[43]

Ashcroft has defended this practice by referring to Robert Kennedy's war on organized crime, when he was attorney general — "Robert Kennedy's Justice Department, it is said, would arrest mobsters for 'spitting on the sidewalk' if it would help in the battle against organized crime." The difference between the two, not noticed by mainstream commentators, is that the mobsters that Kennedy went after were known on the basis of considerable evidence to be mobsters — they had just never been convicted in court. The vast majority of people detained by Ashcroft are not known to have been associated with any crime, other than possibly immigration infractions. A more accurate parallel would be if Kennedy's agents arrested any Italian-American for spitting on the sidewalk.

With the possible exception of increased information sharing, roving wiretaps, and detention of the handful of people being held on material witness orders (those are the ones actually suspected of knowing something relevant to the investigation), these measures do nothing to increase security or further the investigation, and even for those there is the question about whether the increase in efficiency balances the harm done to civil liberties.

Some of the measures are counterproductive. Declaring political protesters terrorists will just obscure the issue, clog up the investigative system, and lessen the legitimacy of investigations into genuine terrorism. Mass detentions are even more likely to backfire. Terrorists who have been detained for immigration infractions have no incentive to reveal information about attacks being planned. And many who might otherwise have volunteered information are scared about the possibility of being indefinitely detained, and angry about the methods that have been used.

In fact, law-enforcement authorities have conceded the uselessness of the dragnet. An article in the *Washington Post* quoted a "senior FBI official" as saying, "We're into this thing for 35 days and nobody is talking . . . frustration has begun to appear." The official goes on to muse about the possible efficacy of torture as an aid to interrogation, with the article saying, "Among the alternative strategies under discussion are using drugs or pressure tactics, such as those employed occasionally by Israeli interrogators, to extract information. Another idea is extraditing the suspects to allied countries where security services sometimes employ threats to family members or resort to torture."[44]

No sooner was the idea suggested than several commentators rushed to support it. Noted lawyer Alan Dershowitz, in an op-ed in the *Los Angeles Times*, argued for "torture warrants"—the idea being that it should be up to a judge, not up to police, to decide whether torture is acceptable in any given case.[45] And Jonathan Alter, an editor at *Newsweek*, wrote, "In this autumn of anger, even a liberal can find his thoughts turning to . . . torture." Even though he concludes, " We can't legalize physical torture; it's contrary to American values," he suggests that we keep an "open mind," adding, "we'll have to think about transferring some suspects to our less squeamish allies, even if that's hypocritical."[46]

This was a species of commentary often seen with regard to Israel, which until a court decision in 1999 allowed "physical pressure" in "ticking-bomb situations." The idea is that if a detainee has information about an immediate threat to public safety but won't tell, torture is acceptable—an idea commentators have supported for Israel and now for the United States, but presumably not for all other countries.

The truth is that in virtually no cases of torture is there a ticking-bomb situation. If there were, it's hard to imagine why torture would be likely to elicit accurate information. In actual fact, torture is used as part of ongoing campaigns to crush political opposition, by wresting names from people and more importantly by spreading fear. Torture, it should go without saying, is a violation of any concept of human decency. It's also a violation of international law.

Of course, the United States is not likely to legalize torture—and, on the other hand, use of surrogates in allied countries to torture non-citizens has long been part of U.S. practice. It is worth noting that in May 2000, the UN Committee against Torture issued a statement concluding that a range of U.S. practices violate the UN Convention against Torture—these include "ill-treatment by police and prison officials, much of it racially discriminatory; sexual assaults upon female detainees and prisoners and degrading conditions of confinement of female prisoners; the use of electro-shock devices and restraint chairs; [and] the excessively harsh regime of super-maximum security prisons."[47] These methods rarely compare in severity with those commonly used in U.S. client states, but they are not inconsiderable—and none of them have anything to do with "ticking bombs," except insofar as they make the people subjected to them into ticking bombs.

The *pièce de résistance* in this crusade against civil liberties came on November 13, when George W. Bush signed an executive order allowing for any non-citizen who has engaged in acts designed to have "adverse effects on the United States, its citizens, national security or economy" and anyone who has "knowingly harbored" such persons to be tried by military tribunals. Military justice hardly accords with normal notions of justice—prosecutor, defendant, and judge are all military officers, and prosecutorial influence is generally far greater than in civilian courts—but the order does not even allow for defendants to be tried under the Uniform Code of Military Justice, which at least preserves some elements of due process.

In the initial proposal, only a two-thirds majority would have been required to convict, even to issue a death sentence. Any evidence that has "probative value to a reasonable person"—that could include not just hearsay but confessions extracted by torture—would be admissible. According to the ACLU, the order could "permit secret trials" and could permit such tribunals to "require less than proof beyond a reasonable doubt, deprive a defendant of counsel of their own choosing, and do away with the presumption of innocence."[48] Individuals who are convicted would have no right to an appeal in "(i) any court of the United States, or any State thereof, (ii) any court of any foreign nation, or (iii) any international tribunal." In response to tremendous national and international criticism, the administration changed some of these provisions in its final plan, reinstituting the requirement of unanimity for a death sentence and making some provision (unspecified) for an "appeals body."

The administration claims that this order will only be used to try accused terrorists captured in Afghanistan, and that the trials will take place on foreign soil, although nothing in the order so limits its application (with the trial in an American court of Zacarias Moussaoi, the alleged "twentieth hijacker," it does seem likely that the administration will stick to what it has said). In any case, it is a gross violation of the rights of due process of any accused. The idea being bruited about that foreigners do not, or ought not to, have the same rights of due process as Americans is, to say the least, incompatible with any universalist vision of human rights.

When questioned about it by the Senate Judiciary Committee, Ashcroft said, "When we come upon those responsible in Afghanistan, are we supposed to read them Miranda rights, hire a flamboyant defense lawyer, bring them back to the United States, create a new cable network of Osama TV or what have you and provide a worldwide platform from which propaganda can be developed?"[49] In one statement, he encapsulated the view that those tarred beforehand as terrorists have no rights, and the reason the administration does not want to give them a fair public hearing—because, although no conceivable defense could justify the acts committed on September 11, U.S. policy would be virtually as difficult to defend before the court of international public opinion. Much better to do away with any potential problem behind closed doors—and it has the added benefit of setting a precedent that can later be used for domestic control.

With this order, the legislative outlines of a potential police state are evident. The chances of this coming to pass are extremely small, because of the strength of various legal institutions, such as a relatively independent judiciary, and because it will set off public opinion, though no mass furor has yet been created.

It's worth mentioning that on the domestic issues covered here—compulsory licensing of Cipro, the economic stimulus package, the curtailment of civil liberties, the order for military tribunals—there has been considerable opposition, even, in some cases, from the ranks of the powerful. In fact, a recent order from Ashcroft to police around the country to bring in and interrogate over 5,000 men, simply because of their country of origin, has been disobeyed by several jurisdictions, including Portland, Oregon. The University of Wisconsin at Madison has also served notice it won't cooperate with questioning of international students. Although the questioning is formally on a voluntary basis, there is a considerable element of pressure applied to the young men being targeted.[50]

14. Racism: We've Come a Long Way

These attacks on democratic rights within the United States, and the reaction to them, have poked holes in some of our most cherished and long-standing beliefs. One of them was that we have come a long way on the question of racism.

There is some truth to the idea that we've come a long way with regard to explicit, overt racial discrimination. Legal safeguards against discrimination abound, although necessary remedial measures like affirmative action have been eviscerated. People are generally far more circumspect in what they say and do, and racial harassment now carries serious penalties with it. Unfortunately, as crises like this show us, much of the progress has simply been in making people hide their racism. This is important progress in itself and has had a collateral effect—there is now a generation that has been brought up hearing only anti-racist messages, including indoctrination through school and the media. So there is a significant minority of young people, aged twenty-something or less, who are remarkably non-racist, even to the point of really seeming to make no distinction. There is, unfortunately, also a significant section of the populace that, underneath, is as racist as ever, perhaps more so after the attacks.

Throughout this section, I intend to focus narrowly on the specific, explicit questions of race brought up by the war on terrorism. Racism is a complex phenomenon, embodying structural and attitudinal aspects. Further, the two aspects are closely intertwined, as each reinforces the other—not only does racial bias help to keep racial minorities from "success" in the terms of the dominant culture, but continuation of such lack of "success" due to structural economic factors helps to reinforce people in their existing biased attitudes. Thus, to treat racism as an integral phenomenon is not possible if one concentrates only on attitudinal factors. Still, what the war on terrorism has really shed light on is attitudes of racial bias in the American public, and that is what I wish to concentrate on.

One index of the nation's recent backsliding on the question of race is the attitude toward racial profiling. A Gallup poll in December 1999 showed 81 percent of Americans, including 80 percent of whites, opposing racial profiling, framed then in terms of differential stopping of motorists by police based on race.[51] Numerous politicians, including many conservatives, had declared profiling to be unconstitutional, a violation of the Fourteenth Amendment right to equal treatment under the law. After the attacks, however, a Gallup poll found 60 percent of Americans favoring racial profiling of ethnic Arabs for airport security checks. Sadly, 71 percent of African Americans were in favor.[52] And many prominent figures have added their voices to that call.

Although such profiling again does not seem to be likely at this point, except informally, there have been plenty of people jumping to distinguish it from previous incidents of profiling because of its putatively rational basis; while African-American drivers are not more likely to be criminals, "Arab-appearing" people are more likely to be terrorists, even if the probability is incredibly small. On the other side, many have pointed out that profiling is counterproductive—profiles are, by their nature, not complete, so they will leave out some people who should be checked; and, furthermore, terrorists will learn to beat the profile, just as most of the 19 hijackers were careful to be clean-shaven and as unlike fundamentalist Muslims in appearance as possible.

Both arguments are true, but not precisely to the point. What most commentators have missed is that profiling is not just bad because, in the case of drivers, it's irrational and involves undue harassment—more fundamentally, it constitutes invidious discrimination, a badge not exactly of servitude but of different and inferior status. The emotional trauma that goes with it, and the deleterious effect on society of having a group of people singled out for special treatment, are profound effects in themselves.

In the majority opinion in *Brown v. Board of Education*, the 1954 case that called for desegregation of the schools, Chief Justice Earl Warren wrote that "even though the physical facilities and other 'tangible' factors may be equal," separating children from others solely because of their race "generates a feeling of inferiority as to their status in the community that may affect their hearts and minds in a way unlikely ever to be undone." Of course, in the case of schools, the tangible factors were also vastly different, but, in a similar vein, nobody ever claimed that desegregating water fountains would make the water of any better quality—it was just that segregation was a badge of inferiority.

One thing it's very hard for others to understand is the depth of anger created in people of other races when they are constantly subject to harassment and set apart as if they are inferior—even though that anger tore apart American cities in the 1960s and may yet do so again. Proponents of a new kind of profiling seem not to have asked themselves about the wisdom of breeding a new generation of Arab Americans full of that kind of anger.

Profiling was only one of several race issues brought to the fore after September 11. The attacks were followed by a spate of hate crimes, with to date six people killed probably because they were taken for Arab or Muslim. There were hundreds of lesser incidents, including one where a mob of from 300 to 500 youths was marching on a mosque in Bridgeview, Illinois, until stopped by police.[53] Several mosques were fire-bombed and Arab and Muslim community organizations got repeated death threats. In a bizarre twist, the New York office of the Islamic Government of Afghanistan got death threats practically every hour for days, even though it was the office of the Taliban's enemies, the Northern Alliance.

Of course, even accounting for all the attacks, plus the detention of over one thousand people almost solely on the basis of race, there was still a dramatic difference from the days of World War II, when over 120,000 people were interned in camps solely on the basis of Japanese descent. This change represented some mix of changes in legal culture and in personal feelings of racism.

The relative weight of each factor can be judged partly by the racist invective generated by the attacks. Ann Coulter, writing in the *National Review Online*, said, "We should invade their countries, kill their leaders and convert them to

Christianity," speaking at the time (September 13) of a generalized Muslim "them," "the ones cheering and dancing right now." Representative John Cooksey (R-La.), speaking about airline security procedures, said, "If I see someone (who) comes in that's got a diaper on his head and a fan belt wrapped around the diaper on his head, that guy needs to be pulled over." Coulter was fired and Cooksey was forced to apologize, but lesser figures went uncensured, like the comedian who quipped on TV that what we need is a "beard-seeking missile."

The responses of private citizens were even less restrained. Some of the responses I received to articles I published after the attacks are indicative. There were the usual "Dear Towel Head" and "Why don't you go back to your own country" responses, as well as "Anything that someone with a name like yours would not like, I will like," an odd response, considering that the Indian government has been one of the biggest supporters of the U.S. war. More disturbing by far were the genocidal ones—the two included both came from people who opposed the Vietnam war and claim to be on the left half of the political spectrum:

> I used to think like you before this happened. Now, I for one can't wait to see the Arabs get what they deserve—to be turned into charred, bloody corpses . . . . If we can't find them we can just follow their smell or listen for the sounds of wife-beating.

The second:

> I grew up as a hippie and anti-war protester during the 60s . . . but this is different. The war in Vietnam was immoral and the USA should never have been involved . . . but when you have butchers from Palestine, Afghanistan, Pakistan, Iran and Iraq attacking the United States, it is time to take armies and bombs and missiles and obliterate the entire region. Then when the dust settles and ALL the murderous Muslims are dead, open the area up for immigration by all the homeless civilized people in the world.

That a self-proclaimed "anti-war protester" could end up repeating, in more extreme form, for the Muslims the prescription that Hitler had for the Slavs, indicates just how deep the well of racism is. Individuals were practically as unrestrained even in public forums—one woman wrote, in a letter to the *New York Times* (September 18), "It is not enough to wipe out Afghanistan. The many other terrorist nations will carry on the mission."

Genocidal sentiments are a fundamental part of American history. Most know of the incredibly thorough genocide of the American Indian, with up to 98 percent of the original population lost. Far fewer know that a Gallup poll in 1944 found 13 percent of Americans calling for the annihilation of every single Japanese person after the war was over. Today, the number would be quite a bit smaller, but not negligible. To see this crop up again after all the seeming progress in eliminating extreme forms of racism is disheartening and frightening.

Racism is important not just for its domestic effects but also for the crucial role it plays in foreign policy. This role should not be oversimplified—it's not as simple as saying this is a "racist war." Although many government policy-makers undoubtedly suffer from racism, some to a great degree, that feeling is not now directly a determinant of foreign policy, although it certainly has been in the past—as gleeful critics of the antiwar movement often like to point out, the war against Serbia was an attack mostly on white Christians to save white Muslims.

The true role racism plays in war is with regard to public support. The public finds it much easier to tolerate the killing of non-white people, especially of Arabs, who have been demonized far beyond any other race in the American mind. The killing of Serbs was tolerated, to a lesser degree, only because of years of demonization, starting with the Bosnia crisis. Even then, there would likely have been no tolerance for punitive sanctions on Serbia that caused white children to starve or die of easily treatable diseases, as has been happening in Iraq, with Arab children, since 1990. As this is written, the toleration of the public for Afghan children starving to death and being blown apart by "smart bombs" seems to be, again, considerably greater than for the same happening to white children anywhere.

Although in recent wars the government has gone out of its way to deplore that racism (unlike in World War II, where racist propaganda was every-where), it is reasonable to assume that this is partly because there is another audience it must play to—the international community, from whom it gener-ally tries to compel support or at least acquiescence—and because a direct call to racist sentiments might very well backfire. Nonetheless the government depends on the prevalence of racism to wage this war.

15. Dissent: Defending to the Death

The racist backlash was hardly a big surprise; after all, it is not difficult to dis-cern the cauldron of racial animosity that underlies everyday life in the United States. Much more of an eye-opener was the attitude toward freedom of speech that emerged from much of the public after September 11.

Dan Guthrie of the Grants Pass (Ore.) *Daily Courier* and Tom Gutting of the *Texas City Sun* were fired for columns in which they suggested that Bush was a coward for flying around the country, from Florida to Louisiana, to Nebraska, instead of visiting New York on September 11. Susan Sontag wrote a column in the *New Yorker*, in which she said, "Where is the acknowledgement that this was not a 'cowardly' attack on 'civilization' or 'liberty' or 'humanity' or 'the free world' but an attack on the world's self-proclaimed super-power, undertaken as a consequence of specific American alliances and actions," adding that the word "cowardly" might better describe people dropping bombs from high in the sky than suicide bombers. She was subjected to a storm of hate mail and death threats. When Bill Maher made similar remarks about courage on the late-night political talk show *Politically Incorrect*, Sears, FedEx, and other advertisers cancelled their ads, prompting him to utter an immediate apology—even though the comments came in the middle of a warmongering and racist rant.

Across the country, people who had tried to suggest that there was a context to the attacks, that the United States had done many things to create resentment around the world, drew heavy fire on them. Several right-wing columnists even referred to them as "traitors." Andrew Sullivan of the *New Republic* wrote, "The middle part of the country—the great red zone that voted for Bush—is clearly ready for war. The decadent Left in its enclaves on the coasts is not dead—and may well mount what amounts to a fifth column." David Horowitz, a leftist turned raving conservative, went one better, reaching into the past to claim that many of those who opposed the Vietnam War were traitors, and that "The blood of hundreds of thousands of Vietnamese, and tens of thousands of Americans, is on the hands of the anti-war activists who prolonged the struggle and gave victory to the Communists."[54]

The Progressive magazine, which ran several antiwar pieces, was forced to lock its doors because of the vitriol coming its way—one e-mailer wrote, "I wish you and Barbara Lee were in the World Trade Center and got your terrorist-loving asses blown up. You serve no purpose in a free society. You make me sick. Drop dead!"

Barbara Lee, the sole congressperson to vote against the use of force resolution, got 45,000 e-mails, phone calls, and faxes in September alone, the majority of them negative and including numerous death threats. The Berkeley City Council passed a resolution calling for Bush to stop the bombing of Afghanistan "as soon as possible," after which it got numerous threats of boycott from corporations, as well as cancellations of conventions planned for the city. Numerous people wrote to say they wouldn't send their children to UC Berkeley.

A high school student at Sissonville High School in West Virginia was not only denied permission to start an anarchist club, she was suspended when she wore a T-shirt critical of U.S. policy. Before being allowed back, she was required to be counseled by a psychologist and was verbally attacked at a school board meeting, even accused of treason. When she came back, she was repeatedly assaulted by other students and eventually forced to withdraw.

Personally, I got e-mails suggesting I go to Afghanistan before the bombing starts, hoping my family (presumed to be abroad somewhere) died in the bombing, wishing I had been in the World Trade Center, and calling me a variety of names.

The backlash against dissent got so bad that even one tenured professor has lost his job because of it. Sami al-Arian, a professor of computer science at the University of Southern Florida, was first suspended with pay and then fired by the university. Al-Arian has been a longtime supporter of the Palestinian cause, and in his youth, even made an intemperate speech about it in public, in which he said, "Victory to Islam! Death to Israel!" — he has since disavowed the concluding sentiment. He has worked for years to help raise money for organizations helping people in the occupied territories, and has been accused of raising money to help fund terrorism, charges he was investigated for and cleared of. Still, when these charges became known after September 11 (he appeared on local TV shows to talk about the reaction of the Arab community in Florida, only to be blindsided by these charges), a hate campaign started, and was whipped up by much reporting in the mass media, including Fox News and local affiliates of Clear Channel Communications, the largest radio network in the country.[55] The university, citing letters of complaint, threats to withdraw students, and in particular a drop in donations, decided to fire him — as a spokesperson said, "Corporate donors report pressure from peers and clients to curtail involvement with the university. Direct mail solicitations have been returned with angry and negative comments."[56]

The university claimed that the firing was not a breach of academic freedom, since it had nothing to do with any statements made by al-Arian in his academic field of computer science. Observers of the affair have noted that the reason given, loss of money and public opprobrium, was much like that used by many schools to keep from integrating in the 1950s and 60s[57] — and, of course, consistent application of such principles would obviate any notion of academic freedom.

The height of overreaction came with a report entitled *Defending Civilization: How Our Universities Are Failing America and What Can Be Done About It*, put out in November 2001 by the American Council of Trustees and Alumni, a right-wing nonprofit group associated with Lynne Cheney. Compiling hundreds of incidents of people on college campuses questioning the war and talking about the history of U.S. foreign policy, it issued a sweeping indictment of academia for being the one sector in the country in which there was diversity of opinion, calling college and university faculty "the weak link in America's response to the attack," accusing professors of sponsoring "teach-ins that typically ranged from moral equivocation to explicit condemnations of America."

Frequently painting people who condemned the terror attacks but also condemned the U.S. response as apologists for terrorism, the report's complete disconnect from reality could be seen in the claim that students and untenured professors felt inhibited from questioning the "dominant campus ideology," which was supposedly the antiwar ideology. It even made an earnest plea that "students and professors who support the war effort not be intimidated."

This public backlash is being called a new McCarthyism. That is certainly not the case, yet. The number of people who have actually lost their jobs is small and there is little chance that loyalty oaths or requirements to testify before Congress will be instituted, as was done in the 1950s. The legal safeguards for speech and thought are far stronger and more effective than they were then. There is, however, a striking and unfortunate similarity in people's attitudes.

The most striking information, perhaps, comes from a *New York Times*/CBS poll, published on October 30, in which, while 57 percent of respondents upheld people's right to hold protest marches and rallies, fully 38 percent opposed it because it might "hurt the war effort." It seems that dissent and the right to freedom of speech are honored when they're irrelevant— either safely in the past, so we can put up statues to dissenters and ignore their modern-day counterparts, or when alternative opinions seem completely marginal, or when they concern issues that people feel don't affect them. On a powerfully emotional issue like September 11, however, for many people that thin veneer of acceptance for difference of opinion was shattered.

In a way, though, the attacks were not a bad sign. People were finally paying attention. Too often Americans have "honored" dissent by ignoring it, allowing people to speak because they thought it would make no difference.

For years now, grassroots antiwar activists, working against the sanctions on Iraq or the bombing of Yugoslavia, have had great difficulty simply in getting any interest from people — the response of most Americans on such issues has been a collective yawn. Once America was attacked, however, many finally saw the relevance of foreign policy to their own interests. The people who in the past refused to listen to those activists but "defended" their right to speak had a very incomplete notion of the rights and obligations of a citizen in a democracy. For too long, too many people have accepted the notion that democracy means simply the right to be left alone to engage in one's private pursuits, with a trip to the voting booth every couple of years.

In truth, the heart of democracy is the ability of the people to affect government policy, even foreign policy, which is generally far harder to change. For a time, the first step in the process of re-politicization had been achieved — people were listening and reacting. For a time, there was a real chance to reach far beyond the traditional peace movement and get an interested if not always sympathetic hearing.

16. The Free Press Reports for Duty

In order to realize that chance, a genuinely free, open, and independent media would have been essential. Even in the best of times, the mass media in the United States is characterized by subservience to power and a drastic limitation of the spectrum of "permissible" opinion. That is even more the case in wartime, and this was no exception. From the beginning, the media far outdid government officials in their calls for vengeance and war. (Much of the material that follows was assembled by Fairness and Accuracy in Reporting, or FAIR, the New York-based media watch group.)

In the *New York Post* the day after the attacks, columnist Steve Dunleavy wrote, ". . . kill the bastards. A gunshot between the eyes, blow them to smithereens, poison them if you have to. As for cities or countries that host these worms, bomb them into basketball courts."

Fox News Channel's Bill O'Reilly, the channel's most popular host (his show, *The O'Reilly Factor*, is proclaimed to be a "no-spin zone") said on his show of September 17 that "the U.S. should bomb the Afghan infrastructure to rubble — the airport, the power plants, their water facilities, and the roads," adding "Remember, the people of any country are ultimately responsible for the government they have. The Germans were responsible for Hitler. The

Afghans are responsible for the Taliban. We should not target civilians. But if they don't rise up against this criminal government, they starve, period." How starving civilians is not "targeting" them he did not explain. His exhortation to violate the Protocols Additional to the Geneva Conventions of 1977, which prohibit deliberate targeting of things necessary to civilian life, like water facilities, went relatively unnoticed.

A. M. Rosenthal, in the *New York Daily News* (September 14), went him one better, suggesting that Afghanistan, Iraq, Iran, Libya, Syria, and Sudan be given three days to hand over all information about links with terrorist organizations, and then "in the three days the terrorists were considering the American ultimatum, the residents of the countries would be urged 24 hours a day by the U.S. to flee the capital and major cities, because they would be bombed to the ground beginning the fourth day."

Quantitatively, a FAIR survey of the *New York Times* and the *Washington Post* op-ed pages for September 12 to October 2 found 44 columns calling for a military response, versus two calling for non-military options involving diplomatic and international legal approaches. Both of the latter were by guest writers, and neither was in the *Times*.[58]

In a similar vein was the incessant airing of CNN footage of a Palestinian woman and a handful of small boys laughing and cheering at news of the attack, images that provoked murderous rage in many Americans. There was no footage of the mass candlelight vigils held in the occupied territories. There was no explanation that this was not the view of most Palestinians. There was no juxtaposition with images of Americans exulting as bombs and missiles rained down on Baghdad in 1991. In fact, the German magazine *Der Spiegel* claims that the camera people shot tight close-ups to hide the fact that the vast majority of passersby were not cheering, and that the woman and boys were asked to act jubilant in return for pastries (without knowing how the footage would be used), but that is the least of the matter.[59]

On top of all these specifics was the atmosphere of jingoism built with artful use of music, the succession of slogans—"America Under Attack," "America Rising," "America Strikes Back," "America at War"—expressions of how evil the attackers and all our foes were as opposed to how good we are, the emotional clinging to government officials—a correspondent even referred to Rumsfeld as a "father figure"[60] for the media—and much more that is hard to evoke in words.

The attitude of the press toward government officials was anything but adversarial. It was not even bland and neutral; the press made clear its desire to enlist in the war effort. Dan Rather expressed it best on CBS's *Late Show with David Letterman* (September 17): "George Bush is the president. He makes the decisions and, you know, it's just one American, wherever he wants me to line up, just tell me where. And he'll make the call." Somehow, he managed to mistake himself for a buck private instead of an independent guardian of the public interest. ABC's Cokie Roberts gave some indication of how probingly military spokespeople would be questioned: "Look, I am, I will just confess to you, a total sucker for the guys who stand up with all the ribbons on and stuff and they say it's true and I'm ready to believe it."[61]

A more quantitative indication of dependence on official sources is revealed by a FAIR survey covering the three networks from September 12 to 17—out of 189 "expert" guests were 105 officials, 50 specialists, 18 corporate representatives, 10 religious figures, and 6 people from advocacy organizations. Of the 50 specialists, only 9 covered Middle East or Afghanistan policy, and they were from organizations, like the Center for Strategic and International Studies and the Rand Corporation, closely associated with the U.S. military. The advocates included some with firefighters' and police organizations and 3 for Arab American organizations, who spent their time "urging tolerance and explaining that the majority of Arab-Americans do not support terrorism." In other words, no foreign policy experts from the left, no peace advocates, nobody likely to challenge the idea of a military response.[62]

Although a few well-known opponents of U.S. foreign policy, like Edward Said, did appear later, and Bill O'Reilly made a habit of bringing in antiwar activists to bellow at, the overwhelming preponderance of the time was devoted to pro-war views. Usually there was no acknowledgment of the fact that there was a question about what policy should be followed. When critics were on, hosts were hostile, cut them off, and generally added to the inherent structural difficulty of trying to compress into a few minutes a history of U.S. policy that people are totally unaware of, a discussion of alternatives to military force, and a dissection of government propaganda.

As is often the case, there were substantial differences between the print media and the broadcast media. In particular, after September 11, there was an almost unprecedented opening of op-ed pages to antiwar views, running the gamut from generalized calls for peace to sharp criticisms of U.S. foreign policy. Though it did not spread to the "paper of record," virtually every major paper in the country ran not one but several pieces taking views of the kind that almost never appear on their pages. However, the vast majority of opinion pieces were pro-war, as were the editorial boards of all major newspapers.

In fact, for the first time in a decade, newspapers were acknowledging in a sustained way the existence of an antiwar movement—a recognition that involved not just op-ed pieces but news stories as well. At the same time, the media embarked on a campaign to portray the antiwar movement as marginal. In part this was a matter of playing fast and loose with the facts; for example, the big peace rally in Washington, D.C., on September 29 that drew from 7,000 (police estimate) to 25,000 (organizers' estimate) people was reported in the New York Times as drawing "a few hundred."[63] In part it involved misrepresenting the movement and its views. The same Times article was headlined, "Protesters in Washington Urge Peace with Terrorists." In the same vein, Michael Kelly, writing in the Washington Post, called pacifists "objectively pro-terrorist."[64]

More common was an appeal to the timeless American shibboleth about left dissenters, that they have no analysis, no coherent thought, and simply react in a mindless, knee-jerk fashion. This was done even by people nominally on the left, like Katha Pollitt writing about a rally in New York on October 13: "Faced with a popular air war conducted, at least on paper, in such a way as to minimize civilian casualties, the peace movement falls back on boilerplate."

And the mainstream media took the gloves off completely, descending to criticize people to whom it would normally never give the time of day. An article called "The Peaceniks Are on the Fringe Where They Belong" in the Los Angeles Times, in order to bolster its thesis that the antiwar movement has nothing to say, actually took the trouble to quote an article of mine out of context, saying "'The antiwar movement has reached no general consensus' concede peace activists Rahul Mahajan and Robert Jensen." This in addition to saying, "It appears that organizers are more concerned with 'putting people on the street' than with giving them anything persuasive to say."[65]

In fact, the antiwar movement had plenty of analysis to give. In an op-ed published shortly after that, my collaborator Robert Jensen and I wrote:

> To many in the news media, it seems we are damned if we do and damned if we don't. When the antiwar movement agrees on general principles, we are criticized for marching in a mindless ideological lockstep. When there is healthy disagreement about specific strategies, we are accused of incoherence and lack of a clear message. Although antiwar activists have put forward serious analysis, commentators prefer to pretend that we offer nothing but slogans. It's as if pundits have decided to evaluate the movement by looking only at the first and last lines of speeches, ignoring everything in the middle.

In virtually all of its coverage, the media chose to reinforce the existing prejudices of the American public about antiwar views as well as antiwar protesters, to ignore and distort the facts to fit its agenda, and to do its best to marginalize any alternative views actually presented.

Far worse, in a way, than the bias and propaganda was the media's self-censorship. A number of critical stories were either not covered or covered hardly at all in the major U.S. media.

The connection with oil got almost no attention, although it was one of the most popular topics in the alternative press. In that regard, the aforementioned BBC story about plans the United States had made in the summer to attack Afghanistan in the fall, was not carried by any major U.S. newspaper.

Similarly, the story that a deal on extraditing bin Laden had been reached, mentioned earlier, was not carried in the United States. Both of these stories, of course, would have helped to demolish the idea that the United States wanted the Taliban to hand over bin Laden, and was forced to go to war because they would not.

Even more important were the consistent attempts to minimize the human impact of the war on Afghanistan. According to an *Agence France-Presse* story (not picked up by U.S. papers), even American print journalists have characterized network news coverage as "jingoistic, superficial, sugar-coated." Foreigners have gone much further—Tony Burman, executive director of CBC in Canada, said (comparing British and American coverage), "It's like watching two different wars. The BBC (British Broadcasting Corporation) has focused very much on the humanitarian issues in the region . . . the human dimension," while on the other hand American networks had "almost exclusively" stuck to Pentagon briefings. He went on to say, "There seems to be a real reluctance on the part of the U.S. television media to dwell on the human impact."[66]

The looming humanitarian crisis was at least reported by American papers, although calls for a bombing halt were largely ignored. The most serious underreporting was of civilian deaths due to the bombing. Of the hundreds of incidents in which civilians were killed, only a handful, like the bombings of Karam, Chowkar-Karez, and villages near Tora Bora, bin Laden's supposed mountain hideout, got sustained coverage. Numerous incidents simply went unreported. This was facilitated by weeks of "all anthrax, all the time" coverage—in total, six people died of anthrax. Brit Hume of Fox News went so far as to wonder why civilian deaths should even be covered—"The question I have, is civilian casualties are historically, by definition, a part of war, really. Should they be as big news as they've been?"[67]

Virtually every time such reports actually did make it into the news, they were followed by the phrase "the report cannot be independently verified," which meant in practice that no Western reporter had verified it. Reports that ran in the *Times of India*, *Dawn*, and other highly respected mainstream but foreign newspapers did not count. Another favorite was to follow any casualty report by reporting that the Pentagon had dismissed those claims as propaganda.

It started when Rumsfeld was asked about the bombing of Karam and reports that 160 people had been killed, a claim he dismissed as "ridiculous," saying the Taliban are "accomplished liars." When reports came out that Kama Ado, a village near Tora Bora, was bombed, with scores of dead, the Pentagon said, "It just didn't happen." Elaborating, spokesman Jim Turner said, "We've checked the imagery, and the closest airstrikes were 20 miles from Kama Ado."[68] Robert Parry, a reporter from the *Independent* in Britain, found the village devastated, saw fragments of U.S. bombs, and at least 40 freshly dug graves (according to him, at least 115 people in that and surrounding villages were killed in U.S. attacks on December 1), but the Pentagon didn't change its story.[69]

So extreme was this dismissal of civilian casualties that on November 24, 2001, after 48 days of bombing, *Los Angeles Times* reporter Paul Richter wrote, "Although estimates are still largely guesses, some experts believe that more than 1,000 Taliban and opposition troops have probably died in the fighting, along with at least dozens of civilians."[70] Given Marc Herold's reported estimate of 3,767 (as of December 6), this was on a par with reporting that "at least tens of thousands of Jews" died in the Holocaust or, indeed, that "at least dozens" had died in the attacks on the World Trade Center. Such a report, if made in an Arab paper, would have occasioned a storm of commentary about the backwardness and lack of respect for truth and civilization of the Islamic world. Richter's estimate, fitting in so well with the prevailing intellectual culture, went unnoticed.

The credulous acceptance and repetition of Pentagon dismissals was all the more amazing given that, on the few times when they were questioned more closely, officials admitted that no serious attempts were being made by the Pentagon to assess civilian deaths. Rumsfeld even admitted that the Pentagon had no basis for any such claims, saying "we generally do not have access to sites of alleged civilian casualties on the ground" and that "in cases where someone does have access to a site, it is often impossible to know how many people were killed, how they died, and by whose hand they did die."[71]

It didn't stop there, however. Many in the media seemed to claim that Afghans wanted to be bombed — "It turns out many of those Afghan 'civilians' were praying for another dose of B-52s to liberate them from the Taliban, casualties or not," wrote Thomas Friedman, the New York Times foreign affairs commentator.[72] Others, like CBS's Randall Pinkston, merely affected surprise that Afghans might object to the killings, reporting that, although until recently "many Afghans" were "raising few objections to civilians accidentally killed in U.S.bombing attacks," the Tora Bora attacks had caused "a troubling new reaction" (criticism of the bombings).[73]

Mostly, the media, when it reported on civilian casualties, focused on them as a difficulty for the U.S. government. David Martin, on CBS Evening News, summed up the attitude in his claim that the Taliban's "chief weapon seems to be pictures they say are innocent civilians killed or injured by the bombing."[74] Again, on November 6, CBS reported that George Bush had "opened a new public relations front in the war on terrorism" because "claims of heavy civilian casualties have provoked howls of protest" in the Islamic world.

According to FAIR, NBC Pentagon correspondent Jim Miklaszewski took it one step further as he "several times portrayed reports of Afghan civilian casualties as an assault on the U.S." Despite the U.S. military's "overwhelming firepower," reported Miklaszewski (October 15), "the Pentagon is on the defensive today." Why? Because "the Taliban took foreign journalists on a guided tour of the village of Karam, where they claim U.S. bombs killed 200 civilians." Later, the Pentagon was still "fighting the propaganda war" by "denying Taliban claims that American bombs have killed more than 1,000 innocent civilians" (October 24). The report did not investigate what a more accurate figure might be, or whether any civilians had been killed at all.[75]

At one point, conservatives launched a campaign criticizing the media for being "too negative." This was partly because there were at least some casualty reports, but perhaps owed more to the occasional critique of the war as a "quagmire." This criticism, that the bombing had dragged on for weeks without discernible result, with the obvious idea that the U.S. government should not be so squeamish about large-scale bombing, was about as far as the media went in actively criticizing government policy — and criticism because the war is not being prosecuted vigorously enough is hardly a challenge to the government.

In any case, the media backed off very quickly once criticized from the right. CNN chief Walter Isaacson, in a ludicrous parody of the journalistic standard of balance, "ordered his staff to balance images of civilian devastation in Afghan cities with reminders that the Taliban harbors murderous terrorists, saying it 'seems perverse to focus too much on the casualties or hardship in Afghanistan.'"[76]

This was followed by a second memo suggesting sample language for anchors: "We must keep in mind, after seeing reports like this from Taliban-controlled areas, that these U.S. military actions are in response to a terrorist attack that killed close to 5,000 innocent people in the U.S." or even "The Pentagon has repeatedly stressed that it is trying to minimize civilian casualties in Afghanistan, even as the Taliban regime continues to harbor terrorists who are connected to the September 11 attacks that claimed thousands of innocent lives in the U.S." Coverage of Ground Zero or of the effects on victims' families did not, however, generally come with a disclaimer that the U.S. government was now engaged in killing innocent people in Afghanistan.

The New York Times reported that these other networks are following a similar strategy — "In the United States, television images of Afghan bombing victims are fleeting, cushioned between anchors or American officials explaining that such sights are only one side of the story," as opposed to other countries, where "images of wounded Afghan children curled in hospital beds or women rocking in despair over a baby's corpse" are "more frequent and lingering."[77]

In a similar vein, on the local level, a memo in the office of the Panama City, Florida, News Herald warned, "DO NOT USE photos on Page 1A showing civilian casualties from the U.S. war on Afghanistan. Our sister paper in Fort Walton Beach has done so and received hundreds and hundreds of threatening e-mails and the like . . . . DO NOT USE wire stories which lead with civilian casualties from the U.S. war on Afghanistan. They should be mentioned further down in the story. If the story needs rewriting to play down the civilian casualties, DO IT."[78] It is impossible to know how many other local papers issued similar instructions.

17. Censorship in Defense of Civilization

And yet all of this self-censorship was not enough for the government, which imposed an unprecedented level of control over the media. After the networks aired Osama bin Laden's videotape broadcast on al-Jazeera on October 7, the U.S. government was very concerned. On October 10, National Security Adviser Condoleeza Rice spoke with executives from ABC, CBS, NBC, Fox and CNN, who accepted her suggestion that any future statements be abridged, with "inflammatory" language removed. This was originally presented as a concern that bin Laden might be sending "coded messages" — a particularly fatuous claim, since even if he were his confederates could always subscribe to al-Jazeera, which is available in the United States via satellite, and see the broadcasts.

On Rice's October 10 call, however, according to FAIR, "NBC News chief Neal Shapiro told the *New York Times* that Rice's main point 'was that here was a charismatic speaker who could arouse anti-American sentiment getting 20 minutes of air time to spew hatred and urge his followers to kill Americans'"[79] —a call for restriction based on political content, not on coded messages.

On October 11, after reports of heavy civilian casualties from bombing of "terrorist training camps," the Pentagon decided to buy exclusive rights to the Ikonos satellite pictures of Afghanistan, a commercial satellite with sufficient resolution to enable one to make out bodies on the ground. It didn't need the pictures, since it has six satellites of its own, and it didn't buy them up for national security reasons; according to the *Guardian*, "Under American law, the U.S. Defense Department has legal power to exercise 'shutter control' over civilian satellites launched from the U.S. in order to prevent enemies using the images while America is at war. But no order for shutter control was given."[80]

According to Dr. John Pike of Globalsecurity.com, an online intelligence newsletter, "If they had imposed shutter control, it is entirely possible that news organizations would have filed a lawsuit against the government arguing prior restraint censorship"[81] because images of bombed-out camps, if they had no information about American troop locations, would not be a threat to national security and therefore could not be censored. It is not difficult to surmise that the images were bought instead just so that such a legal challenge could be avoided. Similarly, one can deduce that the reason the Pentagon wanted the images censored was not security of troops, but a desire to conceal information about civilian casualties.

The Pentagon also severely restricted media access to the war. The strict military censorship of the Gulf War, where reporters were kept in "pools," completely dependent on permission from the military command to go anywhere, strictly monitored when they talked to the troops, and forced to get every story read and cleared by military escorts, was deeply resented by the press, and after the Gulf War the press and the Pentagon agreed on nine principles of access. Three of those principles are:

— Open and independent reporting will be the principal means of coverage of U.S. military operations.

— Pools are not to serve as the standard of covering U.S. military operations.

— Journalists will be provided access to all major military units.

The principles were not honored in the Kosovo war, when control of the press
was even tighter than in the Gulf War. Although Rumsfeld agreed to them in
principle with regard to the war on Afghanistan, in practice even the minimal
coverage allowed during the Gulf War was denied.

The first time a "pool" was allowed to visit Afghanistan was at the end of
November, eight weeks into the bombing.[82] As the *Washington Post* said,
"Almost all information has been released from the Pentagon, far away from
the conflict, and much of it has been dated and vague." In other conflicts,
reporters were allowed to stay with military units and cover daily operations,
but this time, even though the Army's Tenth Mountain Division, for example,
was in Uzbekistan for almost two months, no reporters were allowed to cover
them. Walt Rodgers, a senior correspondent for CNN, said, "We had greater
freedom of coverage of Soviet military operations in Afghanistan than we had
at Camp Rhino."[83] On one occasion, when some information did get out,
Rumsfeld made a point of threatening the person who leaked it, saying the
release was "clearly a violation of federal criminal law."[84]

This extreme clampdown on the press occurred even though much of the
media was champing at the bit to help the U.S. war effort. Cokie Roberts,
while interviewing Donald Rumsfeld, even said, "There's some sense that
we're losing the propaganda war. And those pictures we saw of those [Afghan]
children at the beginning of the program have taken the place, in our minds,
of the pictures of the World Trade Center being blown up. Why not allow
more press access so that the United States' press can show pictures that fight
the Arab press?"[85]—an odd vision of the role of a free press in a democracy.

Of course, the foreign press, some of which had correspondents on the
ground in Afghanistan, could not be so easily muzzled and was not nearly so
cooperative, so, despite the tremendous amount of control and the tremendous
reach of American media organizations worldwide, there was the constant
refrain that the Pentagon was "losing the propaganda war" to the Taliban, a
group with so little understanding of public relations that they did not allow foreign journalists consistent access to bombed areas and without significant
leverage over a single media instrument of international scope. The Pentagon

felt so beleaguered that it even hired the Rendon Group, a PR firm in Washington, D.C., to help get its "message" across to the Islamic world.

Speaking from Egypt, a nameless Western diplomat said, "Talking heads just can't compete with powerful images. The images touch emotions, and people in this part of the world react according to their emotions"[86] — reacting according to emotions being, presumably, something foreign to Americans and other civilized people.

Although it couldn't stop people in the Islamic world from having their emotions touched, nor could it target all the world media, the Pentagon did target what it could, bombing about 20 Taliban-run Voice of Sharia regional radio stations, acts strikingly reminiscent of the 1999 NATO bombing of Radio Television Serbia (RTS) in Belgrade, which killed 16 civilians. Amnesty International, always very circumspect about charging the United States with war crimes, did conclude that the attack on RTS was an attack on civilians, an act banned by Article 52 (I) of the Geneva Convention protocols, and thus that it "constitutes a war crime."

When asked by al-Jazeera about targeting these radio stations (the U.S. press didn't bother to question such a blatant example of censorship), Rumsfeld echoed the justification given in 1999, saying that the stations were "propaganda vehicles for the Taliban leadership and for the people that are harboring the terrorists and for the al-Qaeda."[87] When pressed on whether this criterion would make it all right for the Taliban to attack Voice of America stations, he claimed that VOA was independent of the State Department and therefore in a different category. Whether such a claim could plausibly be made of Fox News, when it comes to foreign policy, is a different question.

Nothing could encapsulate all of the issues relevant to media coverage better than the story of al-Jazeera, an Arabic satellite TV station that reaches about 40 million people, partly funded by the emir of Qatar and employing a wide variety of journalists, including many who used to work for the BBC. Catapulted to worldwide prominence on October 7, when it broadcast a video of bin Laden calling the Islamic world to jihad against the United States, which was rebroadcast by U.S. networks, it had been of tremendous significance in the Arab world since shortly after its founding in 1996.

Known for its free-wheeling talk shows in which normally taboo subjects such as sex, political corruption, and even Islamic fundamentalism are discussed, for its open criticism of Arab regimes, and for its practice, almost unique in the region, of airing opposing viewpoints, like those of Israeli officials, when talking about Middle East politics, it has been a breath of fresh air in the very region of the world that most lacks independent media.

Its frequent coverage of Israeli military attacks on Palestinians and of the sanctions on Iraq have done a great deal to mobilize public opinion in the Arab world. Al-Jazeera is certainly not "unbiased." It consistently refers to Palestinians killed by Israelis as "martyrs," for example, but it certainly stacks up well against American networks, who have an equally biased usage of terms like "terrorist." Even before the bombing started, the Bush administration was afraid of the effect such an independent station might have on its attempts to manipulate public opinion, so Colin Powell actually met with the emir of Qatar on October 3 to ask him to "restrain" al-Jazeera because it is "unbalanced and encourages anti-American sentiment." Among the charges made by State Department officials were that it continued to run an old TV interview with bin Laden and that it had "invited anti-American guests who have argued that U.S. foreign policy was to blame for the September 11 terrorist attacks"—a view that is, of course, taboo in one of the regions most victimized by that foreign policy.[88] Thus was seen the strange tableau of a feudal ruler of a state with very few democratic freedoms telling the representative of the "leader of the free world" that he had an obligation to allow freedom of the press.

Not content with this, on October 7, day one of the bombing campaign in Afghanistan, Powell denounced the network for airing "vitriolic, irresponsible statements"—meaning bin Laden's statements, also aired on ABC. The U.S. media, stunned by the example of a TV station that was actually willing to question U.S. foreign policy and challenge U.S. government authority, reacted with visceral revulsion. Dan Rather went so far as to ask whether there was "any indication that Osama bin Laden has helped finance this operation." NPR warned that al-Jazeera's coverage should "come with a health warning."[89]

Unable to prevail with Qatar, the United States still managed to muzzle al-Jazeera's broadcasts from Afghanistan for some time, bombing its Kabul office on November 12, shortly before the Northern Alliance took over the city. None of the staff were hurt, since the building was empty at the time. The bombing has been reported in almost all U.S. accounts as an accident, even though Col. Brian Hoey, a spokesman for the U.S. Central Command in Tampa, admitted it was targeted on purpose, based on "compelling" evidence that it was in use by al-Qaeda. He added that, at the time of attack, "the indications we had were that this was not an al-Jazeera office."[90] At that time, al-Jazeera had been broadcasting from there for over a month, and, as

Mohammed Jassim al-Ali, al-Jazeera's managing editor, told the Associated Press, "They [the Americans] know where we are located and they know what we have in our office and we also did not get any warning." At the least, the claim that the United States didn't know that al-Jazeera was using that office is hard to credit – especially since deliberate targeting would have been perfectly consistent with U.S. practice regarding Afghan radio and Serbian TV.

As millions continue to tune in to al-Jazeera to find out what's really happening in the Middle East, it's worth reflecting on the larger lessons the al-Jazeera phenomenon might point to. The U.S. mass media, when it comes to war, have tied themselves tightly to the U.S. government. Partly this has to do with the question of access to "sources," partly with the fact that U.S. foreign policy is often tied to the interests of U.S. corporations, and the media are corporations. Partly it has to do with a shared ideology among those who have made it to the top of the ladder—there is a filtering process, as well as a learning process for those who wish to rise.

In part, U.S. journalism has become so subservient, so "don't-rock-the-boat" because of its own professional ethic of "objectivity." In journalism, "objectivity" describes a set of practices developed to certify that work is considered "professional." They include a heavy reliance on official sources, a standard of newsworthiness that routinely excludes alternative points of view, a disdain for sources considered partisan, and a commitment to the idea that stories can be unbiased even when they aren't true. The paradox is that those practices do not produce "objectivity in journalism"—that is, accounts of the world that are as complete and accurate as possible, balanced, without prejudgments. Some of the tenets behind these practices, like the idea of "balance," have a certain limited validity but are severely misapplied, as in the case of Walter Isaacson's dictum to CNN employees. Other tenets, like the idea that official sources are "unbiased" and that their pronouncements are "news" while those of dissidents are neither, are simply ludicrous.

A useful antidote to the standard journalistic framework is the idea of independence—real independence from the government and corporate interests that hold virtually all institutional power in the culture. Those interests rarely attempt overt control of journalists, but they exert strong pressure toward self-censorship and encourage journalists to accept the fundamental assumptions and parameters of those systems of power.

In a country with significant formal freedom of the press, we have ended up with virtually no independent journalism, except in the left alternative press. In many ways, this is the freest society in the world, and yet the spectrum of our political discourse is far narrower than in most of the world. Anyone watching the Pakistani press, which is always at risk of overt censorship, pillory their military dictator while papers in the United States play softball with Bush has to be appalled.

There has been much blather about the "CNN effect," the fact that television cameras somewhere can supposedly affect policy by arousing public opinion in a tide that governments cannot handle. The Arab world has a parallel "al-Jazeera effect," most notably in its newfound political outrage over U.S. and Israeli policy in the Middle East. What we need in the United States is a little "al-Jazeera effect" of our own—a commitment to find out the true story, which seldom happens in government briefing rooms.

18. The People Want War

It is conceivable that someone might grant all of these statements about the media coverage and still claim that it didn't matter, because all the polls showed that people in the United States overwhelmingly favored war. And, indeed, support for the war (after October 7) among Americans has consistently run at 90 percent or higher, as has approval for Bush's performance.

Still, a closer look at the data reveals a more complex picture. First, on the question of international support for the war, no subtle analysis is required. A Gallup International poll,[91] posing sample audiences the question of extradition versus military action, found only three countries with a majority in favor of military action—the United States, with 54 percent, India, with 72 percent, and Israel, with 77 percent. The results for India can safely be dismissed, because a telephone poll cannot possibly involve a representative sample of the country where there is roughly a single phone line for 100 people, not even in approximation. In many countries, the percentage favoring military action was in the single digits. Even in the United States and Israel, the numbers were far lower than 90 percent, because the poll explicitly posed extradition as an option. Presumably, if the public had been informed that extradition had been an option, but was deliberately ignored by the U.S. government (and that it still was a possibility), those 90 percent plus figures might have been different.

Again, in the United States and Israel, 56 percent favored striking only military targets, as opposed to 28 percent and 36 percent respectively who thought striking a combination of military and civilian targets was acceptable. Had respondents been informed that there is no such thing as a war conducted by aerial bombing in which only military targets are hit, the numbers supporting a military response might well have been significantly lower. An indication that this is true comes in a USA TODAY/CNN/Gallup Poll, in which 62 percent said the United States should strike only those involved in last week's attack, even if it took months.[92] Of course, one cannot strike "only those involved" by bombing from the air.

More directly, a poll in the *Observer* in Britain (September 23) found that only 27 percent backed "massive air strikes against countries knowingly harbouring terrorist organizations" but 65 percent backed "surgical air strikes." Again, an understanding of the true extent of "collateral damage" may have made a significant difference.

Another example: in Britain, there was far more coverage in print and broadcast media of the humanitarian crisis and how the bombing was exacerbating it. Specifically covered in detail were the calls being made by aid agencies for a bombing halt so that enough aid could be trucked in. A poll published in the *Guardian* on October 30 found that 54 percent favored a bombing halt — interestingly, among women it was 59 percent for to 19 percent against, while among men it was 49 percent for to 40 percent against. This was true even though a significant majority favored the war, so it was clearly a specific reaction to the humanitarian crisis. In the United States, there was very little coverage of the humanitarian crisis, and no questions asked about a bombing pause on any of the mainstream polls.

Polls are notoriously volatile — they vary greatly depending on the background information given, on the way questions are phrased, and on the alternatives given. Responses also have no requirement of logical consistency. So to draw any very specific conclusions from these numbers would be a mistake. One can say, however, that there is good reason to believe that the entire ideological construct of "diplomacy," "humanitarian intervention," and "surgical strikes," and the concerted media campaign to sanitize wars really make a difference to public opinion. There was in this case a small hard core that would have been in favor of any war, no matter how bloody it looked, no matter how avoidable — there was also, however, a large group in the center that had to be sold on an image of war fought reluctantly, as a last resort, and with exacting concern for civilian casualties, in order to support it.

It is here in this "vital center" that the hope for creating a world in which policy is based on principle, not on power, rests. Had other analyses been given proper exposure, had the case against government misrepresentations been made, had the U.S. media really reported on what was going on, had

people tried hard enough to find out the truth, public opinion might well
have swung against the war.

19. We Have to Do Something

And yet most people never heard an alternative point of view, and others who
did hear one were unwilling to believe it. This war, somewhat like Kosovo but
more so, was distinguished by the large number of left-liberals, with a history
of opposing U.S. intervention in Vietnam, Central America, and the Gulf
War, who supported it.

Instead of sampling their various apologies for the war, some of which
seemed based on no discernible principle, let us simply look at the case made
by one of the most principled and consistent opponents of U.S. aggression,
Richard Falk:

> I have never since my childhood supported a shooting war in which the United
> States was involved, although in retrospect I think the NATO war in Kosovo
> achieved beneficial results. The war in Afghanistan against apocalyptic terrorism
> qualifies in my understanding as the first truly just war since World War II. But the
> justice of the cause and of the limited ends is in danger of being negated by the
> injustice of improper means and excessive ends. Unlike World War II and prior just
> wars, this one can be won only if tactics adhere to legal and moral constraints on the
> means used to conduct it, and to limited ends.

He goes on to enunciate the principles of a "just war":

— the principle of discrimination: force must be directed at a military target, with damage to civilians and civilian society being incidental;

— the principle of proportionality: force must not be greater than that
needed to achieve an acceptable military result and must not be greater
than the provoking cause;

— the principle of humanity: force must not be directed even against
enemy personnel if they are subject to capture, wounded or under control (as with prisoners of war);

— the principle of necessity: force should be used only if nonviolent
means to achieve military goals are unavailable.[93]

There is, of course, no need specifically to refute the thesis that this was a just war—that has been one of the main tasks of this essay. Indeed, as more of the facts roll in, Falk has started to qualify his position—unlike many of the less principled members of the group mentioned. But it is interesting to speculate why this point of view would arise in people who know better. It's hard to imagine that they thought the United States would suddenly start to approach political issues or to wage war in a dramatically new way, nor that they thought the fundamental principles on which the exercise of U.S. power is based had suddenly changed.

More likely, it started with the recognition that this situation was fundamentally different from the situation in past wars (after World War II). In the past, activists who critiqued or resisted unjust U.S. foreign policy and militarism faced three main scenarios in which U.S. actions were blatantly unjust and the raw exercise of U.S. power was obviously wrong:

— U.S. attempts to overthrow democratically elected governments, such as Iran in 1953, Guatemala in 1954, and Chile in 1973.

— U.S. wars against national liberation movements, such as Vietnam in the 1960s, or against attempts to consolidate national liberation, such as Nicaragua throughout the 1980s.

— U.S. wars in response to clearly illegal acts, but where the U.S. short-circuited negotiations and used indiscriminate, gratuitous violence that killed huge numbers of civilians (directly and indirectly), such as in the Gulf War in 1991.

In all those cases, there was no threat to the people of the United States, even though many of the interventions were carried out in the context of the Cold War project of making people afraid of threats-that-might-come. The solutions were simple—in the first two cases, no intervention by the United States, and in the third, diplomacy and negotiations within the framework of international law while keeping the United States from unilateral military action.

But this war was sparked by attacks on U.S. soil, and so the United States was justified in taking the lead in the response. The enemy, though not exactly "apocalyptic," was an enemy whose power had to be eliminated, an enemy whose acts could not possibly be justified. As Howard Zinn suggested, many people confused this just cause with a "just war," making the logical leap that because this time the United States was justified in taking steps that it would therefore take just steps, in contradiction to all its past history and to the continuing imperatives on which that history was based. Part of the reason they did is that they fell victim to the easy dichotomization reflected in all mainstream coverage of the antiwar movement—either you're in favor of war or you want to "do nothing."

In other words, the question came down to the one that dissenters from the status quo are always faced with—"What's your solution?" In part, this question is an intellectually illegitimate method of suppressing or ridiculing dissent. It asks the dissenter to accept ground rules and structures of power she opposes and, within those constraints, fashion a "solution" addressing concerns that are often at odds with what she thinks are the legitimate concerns. It asks those who seek social justice to suggest a way to clean up the messes created by the machinations of power while preserving the structures of power that are themselves the ultimate source of the problem.

Still, we live in the here and now, and to oppose the policies of the day one must be able to proffer meaningful short-term alternatives. There was and is a solution to be proposed, and its outlines became clear to the antiwar movement, if not to its detractors, in a remarkably short time.

The key is to recognize that the problem of terrorist networks is neither a military matter nor solely a criminal one—it is a combined political and criminal matter and requires a solution that addresses both elements. The call made by some to treat terrorism solely as a police matter in which law enforcement agencies pursue the perpetrators and bring them to justice through courts, domestic or international, through international cooperation between governments, though clearly central to the task, was in itself insufficient, as made clear by the outpouring of popular support for bin Laden in the Islamic world.

It would have taken force, if not necessarily military force, to "root out" all of al-Qaeda (although the Taliban were willing to extradite bin Laden, there are thousands of al-Qaeda members around the world). Such use of force, however, would likely have caused more recruits to flock to the cause, and increase the number of people willing to provide cover to such terrorists. Any group like that depends for its continued existence on, not exactly support, but acceptance and camouflage by the population around it. The "Arab Afghans" stood out in Afghanistan, but clearly the wellsprings of these networks are countries like Egypt and Saudi Arabia.

In order to have a real chance of rooting out such terrorists, the cooperation not just of governments of the region but of the people of the region is essential. The way to get it is clear. It can't be done by backroom arm twisting, kickbacks, and bribes. It has to be done by a fundamental change of policy.

Here one can actually learn from the work of "liberal" counterinsurgency experts like those who designed the successful British counterinsurgency in Malaysia, who saw that the best way to defeat movements of national liberation was to actually win the hearts and minds of people (not just talk about it, as was done in Vietnam) rather than try to defeat them militarily. In those situations, as in this one, military force simply drives more people into resistance. Measures designed to ease the pressure toward insurgency, such as land reform then and changing U.S. Middle East policy now, are far more likely to be effective. The U.S. alternative in Vietnam was a wholesale attempt to destroy civilian society—"draining the swamp" in Donald Rumsfeld's phrase. The alternative now would be an unending war, whether by bombing or police action, against the people of the Islamic world, with further acts of terrorism in retaliation.

In the past, such strategies were part of a foreign policy "debate" in which the end goal of U.S. economic domination of Third World countries was shared by all parties, and so they were entirely illegitimate. Now, it is different—these terrorists are not the voice of the dispossessed and they are not a national liberation movement. Their vision for their own societies is grotesque. But they have managed, however illegitimately, to tap into something in the wider populace of their countries.

There is tremendous justified anger in the Islamic world at U.S. foreign policy. For the vast majority of the populace, it has not translated to anger at the United States as a nation or at Americans as a people. For groups like al-Qaeda, it has. Their aims and methods are rejected by that majority, but the shared anger at U.S. domination provides these terror networks their only cover.

In the article quoted above, Falk also said, "Whatever the global role of the United States—and it is certainly responsible for much global suffering and injustice, giving rise to widespread resentment that at its inner core fuels the terrorist impulse—it cannot be addressed so long as this movement of global terrorism is at large and prepared to carry on with its demonic work."

In fact, the opposite was true: after the attacks, and now as well, is precisely the time to address those long-term issues. It is the time for a grand bargain— lift the sanctions on Iraq, end military support for Israel unless it withdraws to its pre-1967 borders, and demilitarize the Gulf region, in exchange for the genuine support of the people of the world in ending the threat of terrorism of the al-Qaeda brand.

Those changes in policy must be preliminary to a larger change. The United States must drop its posture of the unilateralist, interventionist superpower. In lieu of its current policy of invoking the rule of law and the international community when convenient and ignoring them when it wishes, it must demonstrate a genuine commitment to being bound by that law and the will of the international community in matters of war and peace. Such a strategy would not have won over bin Laden or other committed terrorists; that would hardly have been the objective. Instead, the objective should have been, and should be, to win over the people who share some of the same grievances but not the same worldview.

After the attacks, there was a tremendous outpouring of sympathy for Americans around the world, in the Islamic world as well. There was a chance to capitalize on that newfound goodwill to, at a stroke, eliminate several major grievances of the Arab world, and enhance domestic security in the United States by simultaneously removing the resentment that creates new terrorists and allowing it to have a real chance at catching the existing ones.

Instead, the United States chose to do the most counterproductive thing possible, continuing as the arrogant, interventionist superpower and further victimizing some of the most wretched people on earth who, even before September 11, were already suffering from a humanitarian emergency as a result of the combined effects of 23 years of war and superpower meddling and 4 years of drought. In one of the most shameful spectacles in modern history, the richest and most powerful nation on earth pounded one of the poorest, most desolate nations on earth for months while proclaiming its virtue to the world.

Part Two

THE NEW
WHITE MAN'S BURDEN

"I am willing to make a bet to anyone here that we care more about
the Iraqi people than Saddam Hussein does."

Secretary of State MADELEINE ALBRIGHT, *CNN Town Hall Meeting*,
Columbus, Ohio, February 18, 1998

LESLEY STAHL *(on UN sanctions against Iraq)*: "We have heard that a half-
million children have died. I mean, that's more children than died in Hiroshima. And, you know, is the price worth it?"

Secretary of State MADELEINE ALBRIGHT: "I think this is a very hard
choice, but the price—we think the price is worth it."

60 Minutes, May 12, 1996

20. The White Man's Burden

In 1899, Rudyard Kipling, foremost apologist for the British Empire,
published a poem titled "The White Man's Burden." It begins:

Take up the White Man's burden—
Send forth the best ye breed—
Go bind your sons to exile
To serve your captives' need;
To wait, in heavy harness,
On fluttered folk and wild—
Your new-caught sullen peoples,
Half devil and half child.

Addressing some prospective young servant of empire, he goes on to add that, though these "new-caught sullen peoples" have great need of him, taking up that burden will get him only "the blame of those ye better, the hate of those ye guard" — but it still must be done, since the civilizing mission is a moral imperative.

Similar sentiments abounded at the time. In 1898, explaining to a Methodist missionary society his decision to invade the Philippines, President McKinley spoke of his inner turmoil, which made him pray to God, who told him that the Filipinos were "unfit for self-government" and that it was his duty to "educate the Filipinos, and uplift and civilize and christianize them" (as he was perhaps unaware, they were mostly Catholic already). Oddly, God also told him that "we could not turn them over to France or Germany—our commercial rivals in the Orient—that would be bad business," but why quibble when pragmatism and altruism converge so beautifully?

Observers of the most heated commentary emanating from the defenders of the established order after September 11 might be forgiven for concluding that not much has changed since then. Rich Lowry, the editor of the ultraconservative *National Review*, in a piece entitled "End Iraq" (taken from a comment by Deputy Secretary Paul Wolfowitz who spoke of "ending states" that sponsor terrorism), wrote that Iraq's government should be dismantled and the country placed under UN trusteeship, and that "the entire effort would represent a return to an enlightened paternalism toward the Third World premised on the idea that the Arabs have failed miserably at self-government and need to start anew."[1] Conservative intellectual Paul Johnson had a similar piece entitled "The Answer to Terrorism? Colonialism" in the *Wall Street Journal*.[2]

These notions found a more "liberal," hence more palatable, expression in a piece by Michael Wines in the *New York Times* shortly after NATO's war against Serbia—for him that war "only underscored the deep ideological divide between an idealistic New World bent on ending inhumanity and an Old World equally fatalistic about unending conflict," indicating "a yawning gap between the West and much of the world on the value of a single human life."[3]

The rhetoric of Kipling and McKinley served a gross falsehood (though Kipling may have believed it), which covered up and justified monstrous crimes. Kipling wrote his lines just a few years after the British, through their brutal extraction of surplus from India, helped to kill over ten and perhaps over twenty million Indians in the late nineteenth century. India periodically had famines before the British, but it had no history of widespread starvation.

The extractive policies of the British were such, however, that even in good times the majority of people were on the edge of starvation. As documented in Mike Davis's remarkable book *Late Victorian Holocausts*, the British responded to severe, endemic famine conditions through much of south and central India in the 1880s by not decreasing taxes, continuing massive food exports *out* of the country, and providing no relief to starving people unless they worked, because "charity" would distort the workings of the free market. In some work camps in India the worker's rations were less than what the Nazis fed prisoners in the Dachau and Buchenwald concentration camps. The U.S. Army butchered hundreds of thousands of Filipinos during its invasion, and devastated the countryside so thoroughly that the total death toll from the invasion may have been as much as a million. And this is just a sampling of the horrors of colonialism.

In some ways, things are much different now. Kipling's empire is no more, and global power is no longer exercised quite so directly, by making laws for other countries, refusing them the right to elect their own government, sending an army to keep the peace, and justifying it all with an ideology of racial supremacy. But this does not mean that things have changed entirely. The inequality of power at the heart of Kipling's empire still exists, even when it is expressed and exercised in different ways. Since the end of the Cold War, the United States has been freer than before to intervene openly and directly, by both military and economic means, in other countries. More and more, these interventions are justified on the grounds of protecting human rights, of protecting Third World peoples from themselves—a new white man's burden. The war on terrorism has taken this to new heights, and helped entrench it in U.S. imperial ideology.

21. The United States as Imperial Power

There can be no mistake about it—the United States is an empire, the most powerful in history. On any given day, there are U.S. armed forces in 140 countries. Before the September 11 crisis, the United States had permanent bases in 69 countries, but it took advantage of the crisis to spread to several more. Its military spending is over five times that of any other country, and far exceeds what is necessary for the real defense of the country from invasion and foreign harm. If you lump together the United States with its direct subordinates, countries that benefit from the economics of empire but rarely contradict the United States, they account for 65 percent of the world's military spending and have a near-total monopoly on economic and military power. It fights wars on a regular basis—recently, its enemies have been unable to put up a fight. When it wins those wars, it generally puts the targeted country under some form of external control that is primarily if not solely administered by itself.

The United States has spearheaded a massive economic assault whose effects in toto have been described as re-colonization. Underpinned always by the military power of the United States, this assault has included the use of the International Monetary Fund and the World Bank to ensnare countries in an inescapable debt trap, thus obliging them to undergo "structural adjustment" and a transition to export-led development, which involves suppressing domestic demand, mainly by lowering the real wages of the workers, and making their economies inputs to the United States and other First World economies—replicating the economic structure of colonialism on a far wider scale. Privatization of state-owned enterprises and currency collapses have led to a massive re-appropriation of the assets of the Third World by corporations in the First. The U.S.–driven proliferation of "free trade" agreements may just be the final nail in the coffin for any hope of independent policy in the Third World. The mechanisms of control of the New World Order, the IMF, World Bank, and World Trade Organization, are all, though ostensibly multilateral, dominated by the United States.

The underlying logic of this empire was aptly summed up in State Department Policy Planning Study 23, issued in 1948. George Kennan wrote:

> The U.S. has about 50 percent of the world's wealth but only 6.3 percent of its population. In this situation we cannot fail to be the object of envy and resentment. Our real task in the coming period is to devise a pattern of relationships which will permit us to maintain this position of disparity without positive detriment to our national security. To do so we will have to dispense with all sentimentality and daydreaming, and our attention will have to be concentrated everywhere on our immediate national objectives. We need not deceive ourselves that we can afford the luxury of altruism and world benefaction. We should cease to talk about such vague and unreal objectives as human rights, the raising of living standards and democratization. The day is not far off when we are going to have to deal in straight power concepts. The less we are then hampered by idealistic slogans, the better.

This should be no surprise—or rather, the only surprise should be that it was admitted so straightforwardly. Much recent sophistry to the contrary, empires are always about extraction of wealth from the provinces for the benefit of the center, without regard to the rights of the subject peoples. They may not benefit all social strata in the imperial nation—in fact, some of the lower classes have to fight and die to maintain the empire—but they always do benefit an elite. In most cases, the wealth is spread around, both among some broad strata of the imperial center, and among a native elite in the provinces, in both cases to help preserve political stability.

Before going forward with the idea of the United States as empire, we should address one possible caveat. The most visible and economically substantive new developments in the world, usually subsumed under the rubric of "globalization," appear de-nationalized—they involve institutionalization of the rights and privileges of corporations and denial of the rights of human beings, and corporations are frequently multinational entities that owe allegiance to no country. Many have concluded that to talk about U.S. and First World control makes little sense. In fact, although it is true that the rights and power of corporations are being entrenched, and that even First World governments have less leeway in economic policy than they used to, it is also true that globalization is very much about increasing First World privilege and control. First World corporations have an advantage and, in unbiased competition with Third World corporations, generally take them over or squeeze them out—a look at the world's top one hundred corporations in 2000 would find fewer Third World corporations than in 1990, even after ten years of "globalization" and supposed "irrelevance of the nation-state." Similarly, the wealth disparity between the richest 20 percent of people in the world and the poorest was 30 to 1 in 1960, 60 to 1 in 1990, and 74 to 1 in 1997; those numbers, compiled from countrywide averages, indicate essentially the disparities between the richest and the poorest nations considered as wholes.

Some would acknowledge not only the fact of empire but even the desire of the United States (as always, we mean by this locution either the government of the United States or the corporations and elite interests for which it stands) for ever more control and ever more wealth extraction, but still say that the United States is a benign empire whose rule benefits everyone. Many refer to the postwar period as the "Pax Americana" to indicate this.

In fact, "Pax Americana" is a misnomer on the scale of the earlier "Pax Romana." The Roman Empire's "peace" required the frequent suppression of anti-colonial revolts in Judea, the crucifixion of 6,000 slaves (in the Spartacus revolt alone) along the Appian Way, and constant fighting with the Germanic tribes. America's "peace" involved three full-scale wars in Korea, Vietnam (and Cambodia and Laos), and Iraq; a large variety of smaller ones like Grenada,

Panama, Serbia, and Afghanistan; a series of military coups like those in Iran, Guatemala, Brazil, Indonesia, and Chile; military support for bloody suppression of popular movements as in Greece, the Philippines, and most of Latin America; and hugely destructive "covert" proxy wars like those in Nicaragua and Afghanistan—and this is just a representative sampling. The direct body count is in several millions, without even taking into account the deaths due to enforced impoverishment so that U.S. corporations could increase their profits. The term itself, like the similar term "Cold War," is a testament to the implicit racism of Western intellectual culture—the war was "cold" only in that there was no direct clash between superpowers and no war involving the rich nations of Western Europe.

So this empire is as brutal as any other (and more than many), using military force to extend and cement its extractive relations just as others have throughout history. All that has changed is the rhetoric of justification.

That rhetoric is crucial to the maintenance of the empire. No government, whether dictatorship or democracy, can remain in power if it cannot represent its actions and ultimately its authority as legitimate. Since the end of World War II, it has been necessary to justify everything, even military intervention, in terms of putatively universal human values. Decolonization, the proliferation of liberation movements in the Third World and the First, and the legacy of the Nazi Holocaust all made it difficult (though not, unfortunately, impossible) to speak openly of another people as *Untermenschen* existing only for the enrichment of the master race.

The new white man's burden is not always expressed in such crudely cultural supremacist terms as those of Michael Wines. U.S. government officials, for example, are far more restrained in their rhetoric, especially since they are frequently trying to obtain the acquiescence of the governing elites in other countries, and have multiracial constituencies at home to contend with as well. What we find instead is military aggression repeatedly justified by appeals to the highest and most noble ideals, like those of the fundamental rights embodied in the Universal Declaration of Human Rights.

Some are calling the new state of affairs "human rights imperialism," a terribly unfortunate term since it seems to suggest either that human rights are an illegitimate concept or that they are no more than a construct to justify U.S. and Western aggression, or perhaps that they are a term only appropriate to Western cultures. In fact, the widespread dissemination and acceptance of basic notions of human rights is one of the most heartening gains of the past half century, and something to be defended and extended.

But it is true that we are seeing a consistent pattern, the ceaseless repetition of the notion that the West, in particular the United States, has the right and even the duty to attack and control other countries, supposedly in the service of "human rights." The first question to ask, in that case, is what is the evidence of the humanitarian intent of institutions like the United States government. We can attempt to assess that humanitarian intent by looking at an indicative, though hardly exhaustive, set of examples of U.S. intervention on supposedly humanitarian grounds.

22. Assessing Humanitarian Intent: Biological Warfare?

In the Gulf War, the United States (and its allies) dropped 88,500 tons of bombs on Iraq, 7.4 percent of which were "smart." Roughly half of the smart bombs, and perhaps 70 percent of all bombs, missed their targets. Estimates of the dead vary widely—the middle of the range is 100–150,000. The United States deliberately targeted telephone and radio exchanges and other civilian communications facilities; oil wells, pumps, pipelines, refineries, storage tanks, and fuel delivery trucks; textile, automobile assembly, and other civilian factories; a baby formula plant; food processing and storage plants; factories for making vaccine; and much of the electrical power grid.[4]

Near the end of the Gulf War, after the Iraqi army had been ordered to leave Kuwait, U.S. forces unleashed death and destruction on the two so-called "Highways of Death" (*Time*, March 18, 1991). A total of perhaps 2,000 military vehicles flying white flags, containing tens of thousands of retreating troops, as well as a large number of civilian vehicles, were attacked. First the U.S. bombers disabled the front and back vehicles, then bombed the resulting traffic jam for hours. The Iraqi vehicles offered no resistance. There were almost no survivors. "It was like shooting fish in a barrel," said one U.S. pilot. On one road, every vehicle for 60 miles was destroyed, with charred corpses everywhere. This was done to an enemy in retreat and suing for peace. Most of the Iraqi soldiers who died were poor conscripts—Saddam Hussein's elite units had been kept out of the path of the fighting.

It was a war the United States wanted in order to increase dramatically its presence and power over the Middle East. From immediately after Iraq's invasion of Kuwait, the greatest fear of the United States was that diplomacy might somehow defuse the crisis without a war. In his book *Shadow*, author Bob Woodward quotes George Bush as telling his Secretary of State, Secretary of Defense, and National Security Adviser, "We have to have a war."

In order to get his war, Bush resolutely rejected all attempts at a diplomatic resolution of the problem, which would have involved giving Iraq token concessions in return for withdrawal. Toward the end, Iraq abandoned any territorial claims, offering "to withdraw from Kuwait if the United States pledges not to attack as soldiers are pulled out, if foreign troops leave the region, and if there is agreement on the Palestinian problem and on the banning of all weapons of mass destruction in the region"—supposedly, resolution of the Palestinian problem and elimination of weapons of mass destruction in the Middle East was something the United States wanted anyway. Had the United States wished to avoid a war, it could presumably have bargained Iraq down even from those terms. After a final ultimatum from Secretary of State Baker was rejected by the Iraqis, according to Woodward, "Bush was jubilant because it was the best news possible, although he would have to conceal it publicly." When the war ended, Bush exclaimed, "By God, we've kicked the Vietnam Syndrome once and for all."[5]

All of this is well known, but some recently declassified documents illuminate a policy that is not so well known. A Defense Intelligence Agency document entitled *Iraq Water Treatment Vulnerabilities*,[6] which was circulated to all major allied commands one day after the Gulf War started, analyzed the weaknesses of the Iraqi water treatment system, the effects of sanctions on a damaged system, and the health effects of untreated water on the Iraqi populace. Noting that, "Iraq depends on importing specialized equipment and some chemicals to purify its water supply," it deduces that "Failing to secure supplies will result in a shortage of pure drinking water for much of the population. This could lead to increased incidences, if not epidemics, of disease." It further speculates that, because chlorine was embargoed under the sanctions (levied on Iraq on August 6, 1990, and continuing in altered form to this day), "Iraq could try convincing the United Nations or individual countries to exempt water treatment supplies from sanctions for humanitarian reasons."

During the Gulf War, nearly every large water treatment plant in the country was attacked, and seven out of eight dams destroyed. Given the existence of the document above, this is clear evidence of a deliberate attempt to destroy or severely damage Iraq's water supply, with full knowledge of the likely results. This was all part of a larger plan, admitted by U.S. government officials to the *Washington Post*, to bomb targets of no military significance in the conflict at hand in order to "create postwar leverage," because they "hoped the bombing would amplify the economic and psychological impact of international sanctions on Iraqi society."[7]

Subsequent declassified documents suggest that the plan to destroy water treatment, then to restrict chlorine and other necessary water treatment supplies, was done with full knowledge of the explosion of water-borne disease that would result. One entitled *Medical Problems in Iraq*, dated March 15, 1991, states that "there are no operational water and sewage treatment plants and the reported incidence of diarrhea is four times above normal levels"; another, *Status of Disease at Refugee Camps*, dated May 1991, reported that "Cholera and measles have emerged at refugee camps. Further infectious diseases will spread due to inadequate water treatment and poor sanitation."

After the war, sanctions on Iraq were renewed, and administered in such a way that for many years very little medicine got into the country (first, Iraq was denied the right to sell oil, so had no money to buy medicine, later importation of all substances was subject to bureaucratic delays and harsh and arbitrary restrictions and denials), including medicine needed to combat the explosion of water-borne disease. In addition, arms inspectors finished off a job begun by the bombing, deliberately destroying vaccine-producing facilities in Iraq, and until the summer of 2001 most vaccines for common infectious diseases were essentially banned from entering Iraq.

This deliberate targeting, and the restrictions of medicine since, are clear violations of international law—Article 54 of the 1977 Protocol Additional to the (Fourth) Geneva Convention makes it illegal to "attack, destroy, remove or render useless objects indispensable to the survival of the civilian population, such as food-stuffs . . . drinking water installations and supplies and irrigation works." More than that, it is tantamount to biological warfare—creating the conditions for disease and then withholding the treatment is little different morally from deliberately introducing a disease-causing organism like anthrax. And, as these documents attest, it was done with full knowledge, even constant monitoring, of the consequences. The new imperialism involves more sophisticated, less direct forms of control, but is no less deadly than the old.

23. Assessing Humanitarian Intent: Making Africa Safe for the AIDS Virus

To gain a better understanding of what is at stake in such interventions, it is worth looking at a case in which U.S. intervention took the form of diplomatic pressure and litigation, rather than war, and where there is no case to be made that the interests of any people except shareholders in pharmaceutical corporations are being served. One of the most shameful episodes in recent history—the attempt by the United States to keep poor countries from making AIDS drugs available to their citizens—helps bring to light the level of humanitarian concern embodied in the policies of the U.S. government.

By 1997, U.S. and European drug companies had pegged the price of the AIDS cocktail at $10–20,000 per year, far beyond the means of almost any Third World citizen. In that year, South Africa, suffering a major AIDS crisis (current estimates are that 20–25 percent of the population is infected), passed a law that would allow them to obtain the drugs at lower prices, through compulsory licensing or parallel importing.

Compulsory licensing involves a government issuing a license for a patented good to be produced by other companies, with payment of a fixed royalty to the patent holder—it's "compulsory" because it doesn't require the agreement of the patent holder. Parallel importing is buying cheaper imports from a third-party country, which may pay lower prices to the patent holder than one's own country. Both methods are commonly used for what governments deem sufficient reason, and are legal under the rules of the World Trade Organization. The U.S. government routinely issues compulsory licenses to U.S. corporations, for everything from air pollution technology to biotech to night vision glasses for military use—none of them quite as pressing a concern as a plague that might kill a quarter of one's population.

Vice President Al Gore, in his attempted role as de facto trade czar, went to bat for U.S. pharmaceutical companies, attempting to pressure South Africa's government into repealing the law by threatening unilateral trade sanctions. Thirty-nine pharmaceutical corporations, backed by the U.S. government, sued to keep South Africa from applying the law. These actions ignited a firestorm of political protest, both in the United States and internationally, and Gore was forced to back down. More recently, in the face of offers from companies like Cipla in India to provide the cocktail at $600 or less per year, big pharmaceuticals have been forced to lower the prices, while maneuvering simultaneously, with the help of the U.S. government, to control the market. While this was going on, AIDS treatment in South Africa and presumably other countries was set back several years and millions of people died. The U.S. government also attempted to pressure Brazil, through negotiations on the proposed Free Trade Area of the Americas, on its compulsory licensing program for AIDS drugs—Brazil's approach to AIDS has been a stunning success, so it was a natural target.

All of this was done for the benefit of an industry that already has some of the highest profits of any industry. The massive profits of the pharmaceutical industry are the result of excessive "intellectual property" protection and massive government funding for basic research, with the results of that research then being appropriated for profit making by corporations. AZT, like many other drugs, had been first synthesized under a government grant and it was developed into a drug against HIV by government funded researchers. Since Africans who couldn't get the AIDS cocktail cheap were in no position to buy it at full price, the programs mentioned above were not even liable to cut very much into corporate profits. This was done just to send a message that even implicit and potential threats to U.S. corporate profits would not be tolerated. The millions who died and will die because of it don't figure into the calculation.

These are just a few indications of the utter moral depravity of U.S. government policy. One might just as well look at the role of the World Bank and IMF in keeping African children from getting an education by forcing African governments to impose "user fees" for elementary education, the ruination of Africa through its external debt. Now, as people of the Third World face a spiraling crisis of debt, lack of access to basic resources, and increasing hopelessness, the current solution of the United States, as articulated by the World Bank, is to force Third World countries to privatize water. How to compare this kind of depravity with the depravity of Third World governments is unclear, but comparison is unnecessary—what ought to be clear is that humanitarian justifications for intervention given by such an anti-humanitarian force as the U.S. government are excuses, not reasons.

24. Humanitarian Interventions in Context: Afghanistan, Somalia, Kosovo, Rwanda

Yet such is the power of systems of indoctrination that even such clear, repeated indications can be dismissed, ignored, and forgotten, while a single example that seems like an indication of genuine humanitarianism is seized on, made to stand in for the larger whole, and used to justify new interventions being proposed. This ideological sleight-of-hand is made much easier by a curious development in the past decade or so. In the past, many of the regimes attacked by the United States had at least something about them worth defending. North Vietnam, Cuba, Nicaragua under the Sandinistas, were all far from perfect and involved greater or lesser degrees of political repression, but they were all regimes that, for the most part, attempted to enhance the welfare of their people. Now the enemies under attack are Iraq under Saddam Hussein, Serbia under Slobodan Milosevic, Afghanistan under the Taliban—flagrantly unjust regimes that have virtually nothing positive and much negative about them.

This is no accident. The reasons have already largely been explained. The combination of military attacks, a ceaseless assault on popular movements and the left, and an integrated world economic system so much controlled by the United States has meant that would-be progressive regimes know that flouting the world order will cause their own populaces more harm in the long run, even though they seem to be acting for social justice in the short run, because of the retribution that will be brought down on them. The collapse of progressive movements because of this U.S. assault has left a political vacuum for repressive, intolerant, and even religious extremist forces—of course, there is enough blame to go around, and much of it must go to the leaders and political elites of the Third World as well.

But it's easy to forget this complicated, and contentious, historical context and focus on what seems to be the case now, on what often seems the difference between light and dark—on the one hand, the Western love of freedom, dedication to truth, and respect for the rights and dignity of the individual, on the other, Third World authoritarianism, corruption, and mendacity.

While we are invited to applaud the freeing of Afghan women by U.S. bombing (the extent to which they will be freed is greatly in doubt, as we will cover later) we are supposed to forget that, as Jimmy Carter's National Security Adviser Zbygniew Brzezinski admitted, the United States bears considerable responsibility for the two decades of war Afghanistan has suffered. That the CIA started operations in Afghanistan six months before the Soviet Union, with the clear idea that this would help precipitate a Soviet invasion and, in Brzezinski's words, give us a chance to "give them their Vietnam."[8] That once war broke out, in the largest CIA operation ever ($3.5 billion was spent by the CIA and billions more by U.S. allies like Saudi Arabia), we funded, armed, and trained the mujaheddin, whose vision for their own society included the virtual enslavement of women—a fact the United States knew from the beginning. That, working through Pakistan's Inter-Services Intelligence (ISI), we channeled most of our aid to the sadistic Gulbuddin Hekmatyar, who first gained fame for leading groups of students to throw acid in the faces of unveiled women and who later killed perhaps 25,000 civilians in Kabul alone through indiscriminate artillery fire. That that same ISI, still in part a tool of ours, still supported and funded by us, created the Taliban, unleashing a medieval horror on Afghanistan. That when the Taliban came to power, even though we knew their first acts were to close girls' schools and impose a host of restraints on women (and men), Undersecretary of State for Near East Affairs Robin Raphel hailed it as "a positive development." That we had cordial relations with the Taliban government for years (the only governments to recognize the Taliban government were our allies Saudi Arabia, the United Arab Emirates, and Pakistan) because of Unocal's ambition to build a pipeline through Afghanistan—Unocal even flew numerous Taliban officials to Houston to show them a good time. That the sanctions we had the UN impose on Afghanistan were done as collective punishment of a nation for the harboring of one man, Osama bin Laden, not because of any concern for women's rights—and that those sanctions further harmed a society we had helped to devastate, causing an estimated 30–50 percent increase in the price of medicine and similar rises in the price of food.

Or, if we do remember these things, defenders of U.S. intervention argue that this simply makes it all the more imperative that we bomb Afghanistan to "atone" for our previous sins. This is an argument for deliberate historical amnesia—since there is little evidence that our government is distinctly more humanitarian or that the nature of the interests served by U.S. foreign policy has changed so much, it is naïve in the extreme to believe that it will simply undo the evil it has done before. This argument comes up often, as most of our recent interventions have been against former allies (and often CIA assets), from Manuel Noriega to Saddam Hussein to Slobodan Milosevic to Osama bin Laden.

Similarly, we look at the U.S. intervention in Somalia in 1992 and see an excess of benevolence that led Americans to go in, feed the people, quell the chaos, and engage in "nation building," only to be thwarted by the rank ingratitude of Somalis, who had the temerity and the lack of humanity to drag a dead American soldier through the streets of Mogadishu. Our natural conclusion is that any talk of the United States as a brutal empire concerned with exploiting as much of the world as it can is sheer nonsense, and if we are to be blamed for anything it is for our naïve decency in a brutal world.

It is not easy to dig beneath this superficial media representation to find the truth, but it is possible. The truth was that the United States had greatly contributed to creating the difficulties in Somalia, and that its reasons for intervention were hardly noble. It backed the brutal dictator Mohammed Siad Barre, sending him $600 million worth of arms in the 1980s, in return for obtaining the right to build military bases in Somalia, and for oil concessions for Chevron, Conoco, Amoco, and Phillips Petroleum. Somalia was strategically crucial both because of its proximity to the oil-rich Middle East and because of the possibility that it too contained significant oil reserves. The unrest after Siad Barre was overthrown threatened the U.S. strategic position in the area and made it impossible for those oil companies to conduct exploration.[9] The U.S. intervention was an attempt to secure both of these interests.

Even harder to see from the United States is that Somalia was not simply a chaotic wasteland where the only language understood was force. In fact, contrary to the popular image of widespread looting and people starving because relief supplies were not getting through, UN Special Representative Mohammed Sahnoun had pioneered a moderately successful program to work through the traditional tribal and clan structure to contain the violence and get food to where it was needed. This program unfortunately did not accord with the U.S. desire to create an artificial national authority from whom it could extract concessions, so Sahnoun was withdrawn and his plan scrapped by the United Nations, acting as a U.S. agent. When the marines landed, after the worst of the starvation was over, their arrival was the proximate cause of the outbreak in violence shown so much on TV. Completely forgotten is that the "humanitarian" intervention involved massive strafing and bombing of Somalis by U.S. forces. The 34 American soldiers who died are remembered (coverage since September 11 of potential plans to attack Somalia often mentions "payback"), but there is no acknowledgment of CIA estimates that 7,000 to 10,000 Somalis were killed by U.S. forces.[10]

A similar story played out in Kosovo.. There were massacres of Albanians by Serbs and violence by the Kosovo Liberation Army against the Serbian government and against Albanians who disagreed with them. An estimated 2,000 people were killed in 1998 (and 200–300,000 ethnic Albanian "internal" refugees generated), and there was some need for intervention from the outside. What was in question was the need for the United States to bomb Serbia.

After ignoring calls for multilateral efforts to address the situation, in February 1999 the United States brought representatives of the Albanians and the Serbian government to the negotiating table in Rambouillet, France, to present them with an ultimatum. During the whole process, the Serb and Albanian delegations were prevented from speaking to one another, since mutual accommodation on their part would not have served U.S. goals. Again, U.S. economic and strategic interests were behind the war. The ethnic unrest was a chance to turn Kosovo into an economic protectorate of the United States, establish a military beachhead in the Balkans, and justify the continued existence of NATO, nearing its 50th birthday with no Warsaw Pact left to oppose.

The U.S. ultimatum was in two parts—a statement of political principles and an implementation agreement. The Serbian delegation was in agreement on the basic political principle of autonomy (not independence) for Kosovo. The proposal that Kosovo have a free market economy and that all "government-owned assets," including "educational institutions, hospitals, natural resources, and production facilities" be privatized (Article II, Section 1, Rambouillet draft agreement)[11] was a clear indication of U.S. interest in economic control, but that too was acceptable to the Serbs.

Much more onerous was the demand that the multinational peacekeeping force necessary to restrain ethnic hostility be under the aegis of NATO. The Serbs, including the Serbian parliament, expressed willingness to consider peacekeeping forces either under the non-military Organization for Security and Cooperation in Europe or directly under the United Nations.

Chapter 5 of the agreement stipulated, "The KFOR [the Kosovo peacekeeping force to be created – R.M.] shall have complete and unimpeded freedom of movement by ground, air, and water into and throughout Kosovo." It would also have "the right to bivouac, maneuver, billet, and utilize any areas or facilities to carry out its responsibilities as required for its support, training, and operations, with such advance notice as may be practicable"—a right whose practice by the British in colonial America was so onerous to the people that the Third Amendment to the U.S. Constitution specifically forbids it. It also specified complete impunity—"Neither the KFOR nor any of its personnel shall be liable for any damages to public or private property that they may cause in the course of duties related to the implementation of this Chapter."

All in all, it was a call for a military occupation of Kosovo by an unaccountable extraterritorial force under the control of the United States, which would turn Kosovo into a political protectorate and an economic dependent of the United States—something no country allows with part of its territory unless it is forced to. Hidden in Appendix B was a provision that NATO forces be provided "free and unrestricted passage and unimpeded passage throughout the Federal Republic of Yugoslavia," thus extending this state of affairs to the entire country.

The Rambouillet draft was designed to be impossible for the Serbs to accept, thus furnishing the United States with a casus belli. Throughout, Serb inability to accept the implementation plan was reported by the press as Serb denial of Albanian national rights and of opposition to peacekeeping measures.

After years of media demonization of Serbs to the point that they were effectively depicted as part of the Third World, this was only too easy to sell to the public, as was the idea that the United States was the right agent to solve the problem, and that it should be done through the use of force.

This is not to suggest that there are not savage conflicts in the Third World, often involving implacable actors who will stop at nothing to aggrandize themselves. The same is true of the First World, except that in both cases most victims come from the Third World. In 1994, Hutu supremacists massacred nearly a million Tutsis and moderate Hutus in Rwanda. Government documents that came to view in May 2001 show conclusively that the United States was aware that it was a genocide but, far more than simply not intervening with peacekeepers, it actively lobbied to get the UN peacekeeping force already on the ground (which contained no Americans) out of there, succeeding in crippling peacekeeping efforts that might have saved hundreds of thousands of lives. It even deliberately covered up for many weeks its own knowledge that genocide was occurring.[12]

More light can be shed on the matter by considering some of the means used in "humanitarian" interventions. Aerial bombing is an important case in point.

The bombing of Serbia, supposedly done simply to protect the Albanians from Serb massacres (a laudable goal had that been the reason), involved 78 days of saturation bombing, which devastated infrastructure and civilian industry, including electrical power plants, fuel depots, an automobile plant, and 31 of 32 bridges across the Danube. The United States (although it was a NATO campaign, the United States was in charge of all major decisions) also deliberately targeted a TV station for broadcasting "propaganda," killing 16 people, an act judged to be a war crime by Amnesty International. Human Rights Watch estimated that 500 civilians were killed—an estimate the Serbian government says is far too low (they claim 1,200–5,000), along with over 1,000 soldiers. The propagating deaths because of destruction of infrastructure, unexploded cluster bomblets, and possibly large amounts of depleted uranium deposited in Kosovo are difficult to calculate.

In order to carry out the bombing, over 1,000 peacekeepers from the Organization for Security and Cooperation in Europe, who were already on the ground, were removed. The bombing also increased tensions and helped gain support for those Serbs who identified Albanians as foreign enemies. For both of these reasons, the rate of ethnic killing was much higher after the bombing started than it was before, with thousands of Albanians (some of whom were armed Kosovo Liberation Army members) killed in a matter of weeks. All in all, an odd way to react to a humanitarian emergency that had seen perhaps 2000 people killed.

Actually, it is long past time that aerial bombing campaigns of the kind carried out by the United States in Iraq, Serbia, and Afghanistan be considered a war crime. They destroy essential civilian infrastructure—in fact, they do so far more thoroughly than was possible in the past, because of the combination of precision weapons and incredible American air superiority, so that air defense is almost irrelevant. After the Gulf War, some people called this the "bomb now, die later" plan.

They kill many civilians directly. Precision weapons are accurate enough to take out any military or civilian target the United States aims for, but they also miss enough to kill many civilians. As one of these bombing campaigns progresses, and pilots flying high in the sky attack "targets of opportunity," they are prone to making errors in visual determination. In Kosovo, one pilot mistakenly bombed a convoy of Albanian refugees, killing 64. Similar events have happened frequently in Afghanistan.

They generate large numbers of refugees, thus causing more suffering, hunger, and death. In Kosovo, the commencement of bombing resulted in about 600,000 Albanian refugees, due presumably to a combination of Serb violence and heavy bombing (when NATO occupied Kosovo and the Albanians returned, hundreds of thousands of Serbs, Roma, Turks, and others were forced to flee). In Afghanistan, again, hundreds of thousands of refugees were generated, some of them starving and gravely suffering as this is written because relief workers cannot reach them with food.

They have severe propagating effects on civilians. Cluster bombs are heavily used, with the attendant problem of unexploded bomblets we mentioned. Depleted uranium is at least anecdotally associated with increases in cancer and birth defects, but the United States continues to use it in armor-piercing weapons. Rebuilding shattered infrastructure, even if it is allowed (it has been largely in Serbia, but not in Iraq), often requires so much outside aid that countries are placed in permanent economic bondage, with policy determined by funding agencies rather than by representative governments.

The cardinal principles of the laws of war are distinction and proportionality. Civilians must be distinguished from military forces and civilian targets from military ones—and, more broadly, noncombatants, whether civilian or injured or imprisoned soldiers, from combatants. Civilian targets must not be deliberately struck, but it is understood that "collateral damage" can result from strikes on military targets—the key here is that the risked damage to civilians be proportional to the military gain one hopes to achieve.

The essence of proportionality is that the military must risk itself in order to minimize civilian casualties on the other side. American bombing campaigns are conducted by bombing from on high, minimizing risk to the military, and letting civilian casualties pile up as they may, from direct and indirect effects. At the very least, it is safe to conclude that any proposal for a "humanitarian" intervention that involves a massive aerial bombing campaign is instantly suspect. And massive bombing campaigns are the only kind the United States undertakes these days.

If we examine its actual practice it is possible to infer the following principles of U.S. humanitarian interventions.

— The humanitarian crisis is an excuse, not a reason. The United States intervenes when it sees something to gain, frequently economic and political control or a military foothold.

— The United States doesn't particularly care whether its intervention ameliorates the humanitarian crisis or exacerbates it. The intervention is structured primarily to serve the aforementioned interest.

— The United States has little interest in traditional humanitarian and peacekeeping methods, which involve a patient presence on the ground, where troops, if they are involved, defend vulnerable people but don't go out of their way to attack; where local political structures are strengthened and enhanced, not replaced; and where the people of the affected country gain a greater role in solving the problem and formulating policy. Such interventions don't serve the purpose of gaining greater power and control. A massive use of military force, on the other hand, always at minimum benefits the United States as an empire by showing its willingness to use force, its devastating superiority, and most of all its impunity—the fact that it can do this and get away with it.

This may seem harshly stated and without nuance. It does, however, provide a far better starting place than all the blather about the West's special regard for life. Formerly colonized peoples know well that if there is indeed a "yawning gap" it is between the West's regard for the lives of its own citizens and its lack of regard for the lives of the Third World victims of its policies.

It may strike some as odd that the same government whose cruel economic policies lead to the deaths of millions every year (Ken Livingstone, the Mayor of London, once said the IMF and World Bank had "killed more people than Hitler" and Jubilee 2000, the activist group calling for cancellation of the Third World debt, estimates that the debt kills 19,000 per day), to the slow strangulation of Iraq and the death of likely over one million Iraqis, should show the care it does in bombing campaigns. Although media reports of that care are greatly exaggerated, it is true that even the Gulf War, not to speak of the Kosovo or Afghanistan wars, involved nothing like the repeated, deliberate targeting of civilians that was a staple of the Vietnam War or of the U.S. bombing of Japan during World War II.

The conclusion that the government's policies have just become more civilized since then doesn't really hold water since, if anything, far more people are killed through the IMF, World Bank, and deprivation of access to medicine through attempts to protect "intellectual property rights" than were killed in Vietnam. And it is scarcely possible to assume that policymakers just don't realize the effects of privatizing water or eliminating access to drugs — especially as, with so many results of these policies already in, the United States is continuing with them.

A more reasonable conclusion would be that, to play to American and increasingly to world public opinion, the United States government adopts a principle of "casualty management." What matters is not how many die, but how visibly they die and how difficult it is to rationalize it away or blame somebody else. Deaths that occur "off-camera" can be ignored; deaths that occur because of complicated policies can be obfuscated. What matters is "plausible deniability" and not the predictable results of U.S. policies.

To see an innocent person, a noncombatant, deliberately shot by an American soldier or bombed from an American plane, is extremely jarring. The blame cannot be put elsewhere; rationalization becomes far more difficult, if not impossible. This is why news of the My Lai massacre, which involved the murder of 300–500 Vietnamese, caused so much consternation in the American public, even though by that time the United States had been mercilessly bombing huge swaths of Vietnam, killing far greater numbers (typical estimates of the number killed by the United States in Vietnam are three to four million).

To see people killed as "collateral damage" in a large-scale bombing campaign is easier to rationalize. It's easier yet when people are killed by economic policies, especially since those policies and their effects are so misrepresented. Best of all is when the blame can easily be placed on some other agency, when the United States may create the preconditions for death, drive the policies that cause it, but somehow arrange, like Pilate, to wash its hands when that death occurs and say, "This has nothing to do with me."

25. Who Cares about Iraq?

The sanctions on Iraq, though not a humanitarian intervention, are nonetheless an arena where several of these concerns play out rather prominently. After the Gulf War, the United States pushed through the United Nations Security Council a resolution, 687, that reimposed economic sanctions,[13] which included a complete ban on all exports from Iraq and a requirement that all imports be approved by the Security Council's Sanctions Committee (any one member of which could deny approval without explanation—not that it mattered so much, since Iraq was not allowed to earn money to buy things). All told, these were and are the most comprehensive sanctions ever imposed in the modern era, and were to be lifted only when UN weapons inspectors could certify that Iraq was free of nuclear, biological, and chemical weapons, and ballistic missiles with more than a certain range, lumped together as "weapons of mass destruction."

Within months of the end of the war, numerous reports indicated a catastrophe in the making. In April, the Harvard Study Team, a group of doctors and social scientists, predicted that, unless something was done, "at least 170,000 children under five years of age will die in the coming year from the delayed effects of the Gulf Crisis." A similar report issued in March by UN Under-Secretary-General Martti Ahtisaari described "near apocalyptic" conditions. The country's entire industrial base had been devastated, it was deprived of its chief source of income, and it was a country that before its invasion of Kuwait imported 70 percent of its food and even more of its medicine. All of its industry was in desperate need of spare parts that Iraq did not manufacture, most of which were blocked from import by the Sanctions Committee. It took no prescience to predict a catastrophe if the country was kept under a near-total economic blockade.

These predictions were borne out. By 1994, Iraq was in the grip of widespread, severe malnutrition, still unable to obtain any goods from outside because it had no source of outside income. In 1996, after much jockeying and delay by both the government of Iraq and the U.S. government, the Oil for Food program was instituted. Initially, it allowed Iraq to sell $4 billion worth of oil per year. Later, the cap on sales was raised to $10.5 billion and in December 1999 eliminated entirely. Of that money, initially 30 percent and more recently 25 percent was taken for the UN Compensation Fund, whose largest beneficiaries have been oil companies, since in monetary terms they were the biggest "victims" of Iraq's invasion of Kuwait. Another 3–4 percent went for UN administrative expenses, including those of the weapons inspectors.

All of that money goes into a bank account in New York, and funds are disbursed only to meet contracts with foreign corporations that are approved by the Sanctions Committee. This external control of Iraq's oil money has meant a complete collapse of the local economy—the government cannot hire local contractors or pay salaries with the oil money, and there is virtually nothing available for any kind of investment. The government also has to pay high prices for foreign food rather than buying from Iraqi food producers, causing a drain on its funds and destroying agricultural markets.

Oil for Food goods started entering Iraq in March 1997. As of January 11, 2002, $18.5 billion worth of goods had entered Iraq through the program— about $14–$15 worth of goods per month per capita. With the advent of the Oil for Food program, a new problem arose—the United States representative on the Sanctions Committee issued frequent "holds" on a wide variety of contracts in a clearly political manner. These have included (sporadic) holds on nitroglycerine for heart patients, syringes, cotton for medicinal uses, and much more—all for the supposed "reason" that these were "dual use" items that could be used to manufacture weapons of mass destruction. There were systematic holds on pipes for use in repairing water treatment plants, refrigerated trucks (necessary for transport of medicine), and, until December 1999, most of the equipment needed for repairing the shattered oil industry, on which Iraq's economy depends.

What makes it clear that this was political and not because of concerns over weapons of mass destruction is that, as of early 2000, the United States had issued over one thousand such holds, with Britain a distant second at a little over 100, and other Security Council members further behind still. Even stranger was the problem of "complementarity." Frequently, the Iraqis receive insulin but no syringes, blood bags but not catheters, heart-lung machines but not the computers to run them. They are then forced to keep the goods they receive warehoused, hoping that the Sanctions Committee will allow the complementary equipment in. This problem occurs so often that many suspect that it is done on purpose. In response to much pressure, from other countries and from activists, the United States allowed this bureaucratic problem to be eased slightly and, over the course of 2000, various "green lists" of automatically approved items were created. In 2000 and 2001, there was substantial alleviation of the problems of getting enough food and medicine into the country, although the problem is still far from solved.

Although there is great debate about the number killed by the sanctions, the most authoritative results come from a UNICEF survey published in August 1999. Based on an extensive household study, it concluded that from 1991–98 excess deaths of children under 5 added up to 500,000. In the three years since, although access to food and medicine have improved somewhat, the rate of death has remained very high — it's not even clear if it has decreased at all, because the progressive deterioration of infrastructure and the continuation of conditions that breed disease are likely more significant effects than the increased access to food and medicine. To estimate that another 100,000 children under 5 have died in those three years is, if anything, excessively conservative. Given the ratio usually reported between children under 5 and total deaths, it's safe to conclude that over one million Iraqis have died as a result of the sanctions.

The usual response from the U.S. government when this is thrown in their faces is both to deny the numbers and claim that the deaths are Saddam Hussein's fault. It is true that Iraq, while cooperating substantially with weapons inspections, has consistently attempted to conceal weapons of mass destruction when it could. Without fulfilling this requirement from Security Council Resolution 687, it cannot get the sanctions lifted unless that resolution and subsequent relevant ones are repealed. It is also true that Saddam Hussein has little reason to think such cooperation would suffice to get the sanctions lifted. As Madeleine Albright said (March 26, 1997) in her first major foreign policy address as Secretary of State: "We do not agree with the nations who argue that if Iraq complies with its obligations concerning weapons of mass destruction, sanctions should be lifted. Our view, which is unshakable, is that Iraq must prove its peaceful intentions . . . . And the evidence is overwhelming that Saddam Hussein's intentions will never be peaceful." Later that year, Clinton said, after another flareup over weapons inspections, "What he has just done is to ensure that the sanctions will be there until the end of time or as long as he lasts."

Similarly, had Saddam Hussein not resisted, a modest Oil for Food program would have started earlier, although the amount would have been inadequate to address any significant level of needs and would have lessened the pressure to lift the sanctions. The program was also a significant breach of Iraq's sovereignty.

On the other hand, the government of Iraq averted widespread starvation by instituting a massive food distribution program involving a weekly ration that has generally been credited by UN officials as an excellent and well-run program. There is also the fact that, throughout the 1980s, as Iraq fought a pointless, destructive, and cruel war with Iran, spending 57 percent of its GDP on the war, it went into debt in order to maintain a high level of social services and standard of living for the people—this included nearly free health care and education through the graduate level.

The United States, in its partial administration of Iraq in the 1990s, has overseen an actual decline in literacy, as elementary schools emptied for lack of supplies (Iraq was eventually forced to impose user fees). The 1990s have seen the people impoverished, doctors, scientists, engineers and other socially necessary people fleeing to the West, and the evolution of a large, massively corrupt elite that drives Mercedes Benz cars while people beg for bread in the streets—a typical Third World model now brought to Iraq.

While it is true that Saddam Hussein builds palaces and cares more for maintaining his power and his military than for the well-being of the Iraqi people, the United States knew this well—it supported him with agricultural credits ($5 billion worth from 1983 to 1990), chemical and biological weapons (over $1.5 billion worth of strategically sensitive exports in the five years before the Gulf War), even while he was killing over 100,000 (probably 130,000) Kurds in the late 80s. At that time, he was a U.S. ally, so his atrocities were given diplomatic cover by the United States while it continued to aid and abet them.

The sanctions by design throw the Iraqi people on the mercy of the government, because the local economy is devastated and all necessary goods must come from the government. The United States has never explained the logic behind inflicting suffering on Iraqis to get Saddam Hussein to change his policies while simultaneously claiming that he doesn't care about that suffering. It is an overt recipe for a stalemate, while people starve and die.

The main justification given for the sanctions, of course, is Iraq's danger to its neighbors (much less now since Iraq has been heavily disarmed while its neighbors have bought billions worth of advanced U.S. arms since the Gulf War). But, partly because it is difficult to maintain this as a sufficient reason when there are babies dying every day, through it all also runs the threat that, as Madeleine Albright said, "we care more." Bill Clinton, before the Desert

Fox bombing of Iraq, said (December 16, 1998), "without the sanctions, we would see the oil-for-food program become oil-for-tanks, resulting in a greater threat to Iraq's neighbors and less food for its people."

The sanctions on Iraq are a form of economic control far beyond the dreams of the average IMF economist (though they talk about "free markets," what they want is countries whose economies they can tightly control for the benefit of foreign corporations). Other countries are pressured to cut government payrolls. Iraq's oil earnings are simply attached so they can't be used to pay government salaries. Other countries are encouraged to buy from foreign corporations (through lower tariffs and other measures)—Iraq's oil earnings can only be used to buy from foreign corporations, or they sit in the bank, untouchable by Iraq.

This outside control is in itself an evil, no matter what an unfettered Saddam Hussein might do. Not only does it destroy the local economy, it freezes in place the political process and removes accountability from the Iraqi government, transferring it instead to Washington. No matter how heartless Hussein is, Iraqis will not find a better life under external control. Giving the country its freedom is the only way. And yet the shadow of the white man's burden falls over the issue whenever it is brought up. Show the U.S. government's lack of concern for the Iraqi people, its role in trapping them between completely untenable options, its perversion and distortion even of the minimal programs in existence like Oil for Food, and its aiding and abetting in the destruction of a country all you like, people still bring up the idea that Iraqis are better off than they would be if the sanctions were lifted.

26. Beyond the White Man's Burden

This survey of U.S. intervention around the world has shown how much of the ground was prepared for the war on terrorism long before the terrorist attacks of September 11. There is a place for the international community to intervene to protect human rights. There is a place for peacekeeping and for humanitarian intervention. There is no place for exercises in U.S. or Western domination, whether economic or military, under the guise of protecting human rights. It is not that difficult to distinguish between the two kinds of intervention, on the basis of the efforts made to negotiate solutions rather than imposing them and to protect those whose human rights are being infringed rather than causing them additional harm.

To create the conditions for disaster through exploitation and constant maneuvering for gain, sabotage the basis of any effective, democratic international mechanism for dealing with human rights problems that arise, then carry out profoundly destructive "humanitarian" interventions is unbelievable effrontery. To have any credibility at all, the West must start showing humanitarian intent in situations it does not try to control. Independence of the Third World does mean control by their own elites in the short run, which may not always be immediately better for the people (although there is little indication that it could be worse), but it is the only way to a better future, and to one in which the dominance of the First World, the re-colonization of the world, is broken.

The imperial arrogance of the United States has gone to such heights that some progressive-minded people throw out the baby with the bathwater, and decide that "human rights" is a Western concern and in itself an imperial imposition. That is most emphatically not my view. Human rights are a concept that belongs to the world, one that needs extension, not suppression. The point is not that the concept is alien to the Third World, but rather that the First World is no better when it comes to human rights than is the Third (internally, it is, but does far more violation of human rights abroad than the Third World does), and that specifically it is a worse guardian of human rights in the Third World than the people of that world would be if they were really in control of their own policies. The world needs a much broader human rights movement—one based on a fundamental understanding of the neocolonial role of the West, in particular the imperial role of the United States— and a commitment to erase neocolonialism simultaneously with advancing human rights in the Third World.

In order to do that, we must get beyond our own neocolonial fantasies, and stop accepting facile justifications for U.S. interventions. Details like those covered here often come out only after the events are over, and, even if they do come out in time, it's never in forums where they are widely read. We must learn from history, so that we can combat the implicit sense of moral superiority that is so necessary to justify these interventions. This is something that requires positive, affirmative efforts in peacetime, as well as reactive efforts when war is on the horizon.

That there is a need for the U.S. government to fool us speaks well of us. That we are so easily and repeatedly fooled does not.

Part Three

NEW DIRECTIONS IN THE WAR AGAINST TERRORISM

27. Afghanistan and Central Asia

The war on terrorism is not over. Bush and all his subordinates have made that clear from the beginning. Afghanistan was "the first battle in the war of the twenty-first century." Already their sights are set on other countries and new objectives. And events in Afghanistan are not at an end. Afghanistan has not yet entered a new era of peace, democracy, and plenitude.

Although the talks in Bonn to form the new government did involve a token presence of a few women, and women have resumed their positions as government employees, doctors, and teachers, the fundamentals have not changed. In many areas, the populace is at the mercy of local warlords, as brutal as the Taliban but not as good at maintaining order. The new government has already stated a commitment to maintaining a harsh interpretation of *Sharia* (Islamic law), although it will supposedly be kinder and gentler than the Taliban's. As Judge Ahamat Ullah Zarif, associated with the new government, told Agence France Presse, adulterers would still be stoned, but "we will use only small stones."[1]

Afghanistan's need for reconstruction is great—the UN Development Program, in conjunction with the World Bank and Asian Development Bank, has estimated that need at $15 billion over the next ten years. The economic domination of Afghanistan by the United States is certain at least in the short term. One would presume the Afghans have little need to fear the standard U.S.–driven "austerity measures," since the Taliban era was one of maximum austerity, but the IMF and World Bank have already moved to promote "dollarization" of Afghanistan's economy, potentially a dangerous step, as Argentina found out near the end of 2001.

The interim leader of Afghanistan handpicked by the United States, Hamid Karzai, is a former paid consultant for Unocal, as is Zalmay Khalilzad, the special envoy from the United States to Afghanistan. Khalilzad was an open apologist for the Taliban in years past, even writing an op-ed in which he compared their brand of Islam favorably with that of Iran. These are frightening developments given Unocal's attempts to lobby on behalf of the Taliban so that they could build a pipeline from the oil-rich Caspian basin to the Indian Ocean running through then Taliban controlled Afghanistan. These plans were put on hold only in August 1998, with the U.S. cruise missile strikes on Afghanistan. (Some of the "terrorist training camps" used by bin Laden's organization were targeted in those strikes. The United States knew exactly where they were, since they had been built by the CIA.)

The pipeline may or may not work out. Since September 11, the price of oil has dropped to under $20 a barrel, making a pipeline a financial loser in the short term. The U.S. rapprochement with Iran also may make possible a pipeline through Iran, geographically and financially much the more sensible arrangement. One thing is sure, though—Unocal's interests will be well represented in the new government, likely better than those of the Afghan people.

It's also sure that the United States is in Central Asia to stay. The fall of the Soviet Union opened up large swathes of territory to be re-colonized by the West (or reintegrated into it in the case of some of the better-off eastern European countries), but Central Asia was a difficult nut to crack. Because of its relative inaccessibility, it was excessively beholden to Russia in many things, including attempts to develop its oil and natural gas resources—a fact that helped Russia continue to exert great political influence on it as well.

That has changed now, with the establishment of a U.S. beachhead in Central Asia. It is too early to tell whether Afghanistan will be stable enough for the United States to want to stay, but there is a dramatically increased U.S. military presence in Pakistan, Tajikistan, Uzbekistan, and Kyrgyzstan (where the United States is already constructing a permanent military base) that is not likely to go away. This is an area where the United States could never establish a foothold before, and both China and Russia are bound to be uncomfortable with its new presence. According to John Pike, a military analyst for GlobalSecurity.com, "Overall, the American military global presence is more pervasive today than at any point in American history."

28. Somalia, the Philippines, and Other Targets

The United States has portrayed Somalia as a haven for al-Qaeda and thus a candidate for military intervention. According to Somalian interim President Abdiqassim Salad Hassan, "People are terrorized to see the largest country in the world threaten this poor country that has been ravaged by civil war for 10 years." He, along with others like the venerable British charity ActionAid, which has worked in the area for 21 years, has also said that U.S. threats of military action are threatening to unravel the extremely fragile peace that has been built slowly between warring clans.

Already, with its customary lack of concern for the human consequences of its actions, the United States has harmed the people of one of the poorest countries in the world severely. On November 7, 2001, it closed Al-Barakat, a money transfer company that operates as part of the hawala network commonly used in the Islamic world for transferring funds. U.S. authorities accused Al-Barakat of transferring funds for al-Qaeda, a claim for which the United Nations, among others, sees no evidence. While it's impossible to be certain about that, one thing is sure—the closure of Al-Barakat has caused severe economic hardship for Somalis, 70 to 80 percent of whom depend on such transfers from the First World for their survival. Hawala transfers account for an annual influx of $200 to $500 million, contrasted with $60 million in humanitarian aid. According to the manager of one such organization, "Shutting down the hawala is tantamount to condemning hundreds of thousands of Somalis to a slow death." Al-Barakat, the largest such organization serving Somalia, was a fundamental underpinning of Somalia's economic system and the "collateral damage" from this closure may be measured in thousands of deaths. This is roughly akin to shutting down the banking system of the United States because one company—Enron, say—used it to funnel funds to hidden affiliates.

The United States is also playing with fire in the Philippines, where a U.S. force of 600 has set up to help pursue the Abu Sayyaf terrorist group, known in the Philippines for kidnapping people for exorbitant ransoms. Although it traces its origins, like al-Qaeda, to the U.S.–backed Afghan jihad, there is no evidence of links to al-Qaeda more recently. The U.S. presence is a major potential provocation, not only because of the history of the Philippines as a U.S. colony, but because there is a significant popular movement, the Moro Islamic Liberation Front, that voices genuine grievances of the kind familiar in poor countries with very unequal distributions of land. This movement has been involved in a guerrilla war, with corresponding counterinsurgency operations by the government, for roughly two decades.

Many in the Philippines trace their independence not to 1946, when its formal status as a colony was ended, but to 1991, when the United States was made to vacate its major military bases and a law was passed barring foreign troops from the country except in transit and for training exercises. The U.S.

presence is a clear violation of this law, but the United States obviously sees an opportunity to use the war on terrorism to reestablish a permanent military presence in the Philippines as well perhaps as to involve itself with the counterinsurgency against the Moros.

Indonesia is another likely venue for military action. Since the ouster of Suharto and the cutoff of military aid and contact over the Indonesian violence in East Timor before and during the September 1999 election, the United States government has been eager to reestablish closer military contact with the Indonesian government, no longer quite as deeply in the U.S. pocket as it was a few years ago.

29. Israel and Palestine

As Israel's occupation of the West Bank and Gaza Strip nears 35 years, the area remains critical for U.S. policy in the region and a major potential flashpoint for national and international tension. Shortly after September 11, when there was serious concern about getting the cooperation of Muslim nations for the war on Afghanistan, the Bush administration took several steps to appear as if it was trying to seek a new solution to the problem of the occupied territories. Bush went so far as to use the word "Palestine" in a speech before the United Nations on November 10, 2001.

Media spin aside, the whole initiative was an attempt to pour old wine into new bottles. As reported in the press, the essence of Bush's position was that if Arafat recognized Israel's right to exist, both parties could get back to the negotiating table. The historical amnesia of both press and public was very useful in this. Apparently no one remembered that Arafat had made a speech to the General Assembly of the UN in 1998 in which he recognized that right and renounced the use of terrorism.

The negotiation Bush said he wanted to restore is the so-called Oslo process,[2] which had been heavily disrupted by the so-called al-Aqsa intifada, the major Palestinian uprising that began on September 28, 2000, and continues as of this writing. The Oslo process was about the Palestinians bargaining away part of their internationally recognized rights to the whole of the occupied territories.

It was designed to take advantage of the fact that after the Gulf War the PLO had virtually no support from Arab governments and no independent power base. As long as it was sitting at a negotiating table instead of organizing political movements and protest, it didn't have a card to play. And so, while both parties talked about negotiating Israeli withdrawal and "final status," on the ground Israel actually increased the rate of settlement by over 50 percent, with the total settler population doubling in the past decade. These settlements are a state-subsidized attempt to annex part of the occupied territories, and are a blatant violation of international law.

On the Palestinian side, Oslo is a recognition of powerlessness. On the Israeli side, it represents recognition of the so-called demographic problem—the occupied territories can't be entirely annexed, because then Israel would either have to give its residents democratic rights and lose the Jewish nature of the state or it would have to institute a legal de jure system of apartheid in place of the *de facto* system it has now. Since neither option is tenable for the current Israeli power structure (the second would dramatically increase international pressure and make it difficult for the United States to keep up its $3 billion a year subsidy to Israel), it has long been recognized that some sort of withdrawal from part of the occupied territories is necessary. A typical representative of the various Israeli political plans, the 1968 Allon plan, called for the eventual annexation of roughly 40 percent of the West Bank.

Israel designed its concessions to allow it to take much of the land of the occupied territories, with its agricultural and other resources, while leaving the crowded, largely ungovernable, city centers to the Palestinian Authority, which would, presumably, have to act as a miniature client state of Israel. In addition to the increased rate of settlement building, Israel constructed a series of bypass roads and military checkpoints—currently, the West Bank is parceled into 220 discrete areas, all of which are sometimes isolated from each other under the increasingly frequent closures levied by Israel.

This perfect device for Israel to take what it wanted while appearing to make concessions was very frustrating for the Palestinians. That frustration boiled over into open rage when Ariel Sharon visited what the Jews call the Temple Mount and the Muslims call the Haram al-Sharif, the third most holy spot in the world for Muslims after Mecca and Medina—with a large, heavily armed security contingent. Sharon is guilty of war crimes in, among other operations, the 1953 massacre in Qibya (69 civilians, mostly women and children, were killed by Israeli Defense Forces personnel blowing up their houses) and the 1982 invasion of southern Lebanon (among other things, he allowed and facilitated the massacres in the Sabra and Shatila refugee camps, carried out by the Lebanese Phalangists, in which anywhere from 800 to 2000 people were killed). Since the beginning of the second intifada, more than 850 Palestinians and 230 Israelis have been killed — the Israelis mostly by a major increase in suicide bombings of civilian areas in Israel carried out by Hamas.

Israel's occupation and settlement activities are in blatant violation of the Fourth Geneva Convention. The activities of its security forces in the occupied territories constitute a constant and severe human rights violation, attested to by every reputable international human rights group. Since the beginning of the second intifada, closures as a form of collective punishment as well as attacks on civilian areas with artillery, tanks, helicopter gunships, and, on a few occasions, even F-16s, have become commonplace. Essentially, Palestinians are living under siege.

After September 11, Israel took advantage of the fact that the world's focus was elsewhere to step up its brutality in the occupied territories and to step up the rhetoric as well, with Prime Minister Ariel Sharon calling Arafat "our bin Laden." While calling for Arafat to stop the violence, it has intentionally made this impossible for him to do. On at least two occasions, it has disrupted agreements between Hamas and the Palestinian Authority for a temporary halt to the violence, once on November 23 by assassinating a Hamas leader, Mahmoud Abu Hanoud. (Assassination is a common and openly admitted Israeli tactic in the occupied territories and is carried out by the Israeli military.) Its military "retaliations" for terrorist attacks have generally targeted the Palestinian Authority's security forces, the very people who are supposed to arrest the terrorists. In fact, Abu Hanoud was at large because Israel attempted to assassinate him with an air strike while the PA held him in prison, only to botch the job, and allowed him to escape instead.

Abu Hanoud's assassination led to several revenge bombings by Hamas, killing over 30 civilians. After these bombings, the United States stopped even its token protestations (particularly hypocritical given that the weapons Israel uses in its military assaults are made in the United States) at Israeli military attacks, leaving Sharon and other hawks a free hand to do as they liked in the occupied territories.

Because of the war on terrorism, the danger to Palestinians has increased dramatically. Even before September 11, Israel had made plans for a military assault on the occupied territories (presented to the Israeli cabinet on July 9, 2001) in which, it was estimated, up to 300 Israelis as well as many thousands of Palestinians might die. Though the attack might well occasion the sending of an international peacekeeping force (a proposal that comes up often in the Security Council, but is always vetoed by the United States), such a force would, the report concluded, be presented with a "fait accompli."

Sharon's strategy of attacking the Palestinian Authority gives Hamas more of a free rein and thus makes it easier for Hamas to continue to disrupt ceasefires by violence. All of this points to a deliberate strategy of preparing the ground for a serious Israeli assault in the near future—an assault that would be justified to the world as an antiterrorism measure. The likelihood of such an attack was made all the greater by an Israeli seizure in early January of a ship it says was carrying 50 tons of arms destined for the Palestinian Authority. Since that time, the United States has openly speculated about cutting off relations with the PA. Arafat denies any knowledge of the shipment. Whether or not the PA was involved, as yet there has been no acknowledgment in the mainstream U.S. media that a people regularly under attack by helicopters, tanks, and fighter planes has a right to get weapons to defend itself.

Hamas's role in any plans for future attacks could be to continue its execrable policy of killing Israeli civilians until Israeli public opinion could justify some kind of invasion—already, since the beginning of the al-Aqsa intifada, public opinion in Israel has swung from a readiness to give back the Palestinians' land in return for security to a desire for some kind of (unspecified) military solution. Even if such an attack does not occur, violence in Israel and Palestine is likely to increase, as is the already unbearable level of oppression and control of Palestinians by Israel.

30. Iraq

Above and beyond all other countries, there is always Iraq, the once and future target. Since 1991, the United States has subjected the country to one form of attack or another, never really needing an excuse to drop a few bombs. As this is written, American and British planes continue their illegal daily overflights by fighter planes of northern and southern Iraq, patrolling the so-called no-fly zones instituted in 1991 (northern) and 1992 (southern) as an act of naked imperial arrogance, unauthorized by any Security Council resolution. Since the U.S. Desert Fox bombing campaign of December 1998, Iraq has made a regular practice of locking its targeting radar onto planes, and often firing at them, what would be considered an act of self-defense by any other country. According to a report by former UN Coordinator of the Humanitarian Program for Iraq Hans von Sponeck, retaliatory attacks from American and British planes, which occur frequently, have killed hundreds of Iraqi civilians, wounded many others, and caused serious economic harm.

After September 11, there was an explosion of calls in the press to attack Iraq, to remove Saddam Hussein from power. Since the Afghanistan campaign has essentially wound up, most proposals suggest a similar model in Iraq, although the Iraqi opposition is much smaller than the Northern Alliance and not well armed. An identifiable group of Iraq hawks has formed, including Richard Perle, chairman of the Defense Advisory Board, a private group that advises Bush, Paul Wolfowitz, Deputy Secretary of Defense, ex-CIA chief James Woolsey, and others.

Most of those calls were centered on claims that there was some link between Iraq and terrorist acts on U.S. soil, although from near the beginning there were some who wrote that Iraq should be attacked whether or not any connection could be shown. The attempts to link Iraq to the anthrax letters, wildly implausible from the beginning, have not panned out. The spores in the letters have been found to be a perfect match for spores manufactured at the Dugway Proving Ground in Utah, a finding that also involved the first public revelation that the United States is manufacturing weapons-grade anthrax.[3]

Attempts to link Iraq to the September 11 attacks hinged on a supposed meeting in Prague between Mohammed Atta, thought to be the ringleader of the terrorists involved in the attacks, and an agent of Iraqi intelligence. Czech security forces went back and forth on whether the meeting occurred. In the *New York Times* of October 20, it was reported that the chairman of the Czech parliamentary defense committee had said, "I haven't seen any direct evidence that Mr. Atta met any Iraqi agent." On October 27, the same paper reports the Czech Interior Minister saying the meeting had taken place.[4] Evidence of U.S. pressure on the Czechs was so clear that even the *Times* speculated on it. Later, on December 17, 2001, Czech police indicated that they had no clear evidence of the meeting, although Atta had entered the country twice in 2000. The link was so tenuous that even U.S. officials had stopped mentioning it several weeks earlier.

On November 19, the administration publicly accused several nations, including Iraq, North Korea, and possibly Iran, of violating the Biological and Toxin Weapons Convention (BTWC), talking further of a need to establish extradition procedures for those who use biological weapons. Although the claim is likely true of Iraq, it is not news—it's been known ever since 1995. It's not difficult to guess that the claim was part of establishing a pretext for a large-scale attack on Iraq.

On November 26, Bush once again sent a message that Iraq's refusal to allow weapons inspectors into the country was a threat and would be punished severely, saying when asked to specify what action would be taken, "he'll [Saddam] find out." Weapons inspectors were withdrawn from Iraq by the Clinton administration in December 1998 in preparation for the "Desert Fox" bombing campaign. The issue had long lain dormant because of Iraq's refusal to allow them in under any circumstances, and Bush's invocation of it was clearly part of a short-term drive to war.

The United States has been held back from attacking because of an almost complete lack of support from traditional allies, although it has achieved some success in winning over the United Kingdom and Turkey (from whose Incirlik air base the United States regularly launches its air patrols and bombing of northern Iraq). Saudi Arabia in particular is dead set against such an attack, and will not allow use of U.S. bases there as a staging area for an attack.

Such an attack, if it came, would be a clear violation of international law and a tremendous affliction for the Iraqis—neither of which considerations has ever given the United States much pause if it felt it could control any backlash from public and world opinion. Furthermore, there is reason to believe that Saddam Hussein would not give up easily, so the war might well rip the already wounded country apart again. Finally, the United States has always made it clear that it has no interest in democracy or any kind of popularly representative government in Iraq.

After the Gulf War, President Bush made an appeal to the Iraqis to rise up and overthrow their repressive government. They did exactly that. Within days, returning Iraqi soldiers ignited a full-scale rebellion in southern Iraq, involving both Shia and Sunni Muslims, which led rapidly to the liberation of several cities. Weeks afterward, Kurds in northern Iraq rose up, similarly liberating several cities. The occupying U.S. Army, which had grounded all Iraqi military flights, lifted its prohibition to allow Saddam Hussein's government to use its helicopter gunships to mow down the rebels—with U.S. fighter planes flying overhead. In his semi-autobiographical book written with Brent Scowcroft, *A World Transformed*, George Bush admitted this and called it a "mistake," but said that it was done because General Schwarzkopf had allowed it already and Bush didn't want to undercut him—an interesting reason for allowing the butchery of tens of thousands of people that Bush himself had called on to rise against Saddam. The U.S. Army also seized arsenals of weapons before the rebels could get to them, and even allowed elite army units still loyal to Hussein to pass through U.S.–occupied territory to retake Basra in southern Iraq.

The conventional justifications for this policy were that the United States had no mandate to interfere in Iraq's internal affairs (although it had already interpreted its mandate to get Iraq out of Kuwait rather liberally, as license to bombard virtually all of Iraq, keeping it up even as Iraqi troops fled the country), and that there was a danger of the country's breaking up, with a Shia southern Iraq possibly aligning with Iran. The United States certainly did not want the country breaking up, but even more important was keeping a popular movement from coming to power.

As Richard Haas, director for Near East Affairs on the National Security Council, said a day after the ceasefire, "Our policy is to get rid of Saddam, not his regime."[5] Brent Scowcroft, then National Security Adviser, later told ABC TV, "I frankly wished [the uprising hadn't happened. I envisioned a postwar government being a military government . . . It's the colonel with the brigade patrolling his palace that's going to get him [Saddam] if someone gets him."[6]

The same concerns played out during CIA operations in 1991–96 in Iraq, constantly designed to instigate a military coup against Saddam, instead of supporting a larger popular movement or uprising. In the Middle East, the United States has traditionally tried to prop up governments that have little popular base, so are dependent on U.S. military aid to stay in control and that keep the lion's share of the oil profits for the benefit only of a small upper stratum. Any large popular movement that tries to take the reins of government out of the hands of such an elite is a tremendous threat to U.S. control. As *New York Times* foreign affairs analyst Thomas Friedman wrote, "Bush never supported the Kurdish and Shiite rebellions against Saddam, or for that matter any democracy movement in Iraq" because he felt that "sanctions would force Saddam's generals to bring him down, and then Washington would have the best of all worlds: an iron-fisted Iraqi junta without Saddam Hussein."[7] Though such a bombing campaign would inevitably be sold to the U.S. public as in the interest of the Iraqi people, the last thing they need is a new iron-fisted junta.

If it decides it can't bomb Iraq, the administration's next move will be to try to push through its "smart sanctions" plan. Although it has been talked about for some time, the first formal proposal was made to the Security Council by the United Kingdom (with U.S. backing) in May 2001.

The plan has been presented as a way to address critical humanitarian concerns in Iraq. Instead of the cumbersome bureaucratic review process now in place, in which the Sanctions Committee must approve any item that is not already on a list of approved goods, the new procedures would automatically allow in all items that are not on a proposed goods review list. The idea is that all the goods that people need to live will get through, while the equipment Saddam wants to rebuild his military will still be denied. Thus, as a British diplomat told reporters, "If our proposals are adopted by the Security Council, Iraq will have no excuse for the suffering of the Iraqi people."[8]

In fact, the proposed changes are nowhere near what is needed. As *The Economist*, the conservative British weekly, said, "The British proposal of 'smart sanctions' offers an aspirin where surgery is called for."[9] According to Human Rights Watch, "An emergency commodity assistance program like oil-for-food, no matter how well funded or well run, cannot reverse the devastating consequences of war and then ten years of virtual shut-down of Iraq's economy."[10]

The problem, as mentioned before, is external control of Iraq's economy. The local economy has collapsed, along with the exchange rate, because, except for a small amount of smuggling, no oil money is flowing into the economy. None of this would be addressed by the new proposals. At this point, the real problem is not so much a need for more influx of consumer goods, but for rebuilding of Iraq's industrial base and reinflation of its economy, something that will be almost impossible while external control continues. And, in fact, the Iraqi government bureaucracy is no longer capable of dealing with the current flow of goods — as the Secretary-General reported in May 2001, "With the increased funding level and the growing magnitude and scope of the programme, the whole tedious and time-consuming process of the preparation and approval of the distribution plan and its annexes are no longer in step with current realities."[11] These concerns are well understood by those proposing it. The London *Daily Telegraph* quotes one anonymous British official saying, "It may be that all there will be is a change of presentation to re-focus domestic and international opinion on Saddam."[12]

There are two prongs to the smart sanctions idea. One is to win the war for public opinion, by putting (in the eyes of the world) the onus for the suffering of Iraqi children completely on the government of Iraq instead of on the U.S. government. This is in response to the widespread perception that, as U.S. officials put it, Saddam has won the "propaganda war" (odd considering the near monopoly of the United States government point of view in the major media and the crudity of Iraqi government propaganda). Colin Powell put it this way: "Saddam Hussein and the Iraqi regime had successfully put the burden on us as denying the wherewithal for civilians and children in Iraq to live and to get the nutrition and the health care they needed," implying that there was no truth to this point of view, but that the United States was helpless before Saddam Hussein's media savvy, as it was later to be before that of the Taliban.[13]

If this was all there was to it, then the fact that smart sanctions only slightly ameliorates the problem instead of solving it would hardly be a reason to oppose them. The other prong, however, is vastly greater control of Iraq's borders, an extension of the current external control paradigm (the United States already exerts some control through a multinational naval blockade that enforces the sanctions, but control of land borders is much more difficult). The official justification is to end smuggling (perhaps $1.5 billion per year enters Iraq through smuggling), both of oil out and of military equipment in.

Forcing Iraq to send the smuggled oil through legal channels would reduce Iraq's total revenue, since 25 percent would be taken for the UN Compensation Fund. More significantly, as Hans von Sponeck and Denis Halliday, both former UN Humanitarian Coordinators for Iraq who resigned in protest of the sanctions, reported, some of the smuggling money goes to pay doctors and other skilled people a higher wage—crucial, since sanctions have caused a phenomenal "brain drain" from Iraq and money obtained under the Oil for Food program cannot be used for salaries or operating expenses of government programs, but only for commodities acquired from abroad. On the other hand, the government of Iraq's ability to smuggle military equipment would be limited.

The extensive monitoring and inspections on Iraq's land borders proposed would presumably involve the U.S. military working with Iraq's neighbors, thus leading to a significantly enhanced U.S. presence in the region, and thus to greater control by the United States. The policy of smart sanctions is partly a response to the growing unrest in the Arab world regarding the suffering of the people of Iraq, partly fueled by al-Jazeera broadcasts prominently featuring the sanctions, and to the growing unity in the Arab world engendered by the Palestinians' al-Aqsa intifada—both developments unfavorable to United States control of the region. In a way, smart sanctions is an attempt to rebuild the "Gulf War coalition," isolating Iraq even more and putting the Middle East in U.S. hands.

The only way out for the Iraqi people is for the sanctions to be lifted, and real control of Iraq's economy put back in Iraqi hands. Security concerns need to be addressed at a regional level—with all of its neighbors armed to the teeth, in large part by a tremendous influx of U.S. arms, calls for Iraq to disarm completely are unfair and unrealistic. The same resolution that reimposed the sanctions after the Gulf War calls, in its preamble, for the establishment of the Middle East as a zone free of weapons of mass destruction.

The current policy actually helps to prop up Saddam Hussein's regime, by enabling him to blame all Iraq's woes on the United States. Iraq might not democratize tomorrow if it is freed from Saddam's dictatorship today. But it is folly to think that a policy of external control that explicitly props up a dictatorial regime is any way to foster democracy. Nor would democracy be fostered by a war to unseat Saddam Hussein and replace him with some junta.

31. Weapons of Mass Destruction as a Casus Belli

Bush's warning to Saddam Hussein, in which he attempted to equate ownership of weapons of mass destruction (WMD) with terrorism, was just one incident in a strong recent trend—an ongoing attempt by the United States to establish the "right" to attack nations simply based on their possession of WMD.

The United States seems never to be at a loss for a reason why an act of aggression is really self-defense. After its brutal invasion of Panama, which involved the shelling for hours of a lower-class civilian neighborhood and killed perhaps 1,000–4,000 people, it informed the world that the invasion was justified under Article 51 of the UN Charter (the article allowing military action in self-defense) so that they could prevent the "territory from being used as a base for smuggling drugs into the United States"[14]—a remarkably novel interpretation that would allow virtually any county to invade another, and would certainly allow many to invade the United States, which has a long history of promoting drug smuggling in covert operations.

Still, the attempt to systematize the mere possession of WMD as a justification for aggression against a country is important not just in the abstract but because it is likely to play an increasingly large role in future U.S. military interventions. The basic idea is not new—when China developed the nuclear bomb in 1964, the United States considered bombing weapons production facilities, with the cooperation of the Soviet Union. Israel's 1981 bombing of Iraq's Osirak nuclear reactor was ostensibly because of concern that Iraq would use the reactor in developing a nuclear bomb.

What's new is that the United States seems to be attempting to institutionalize it. The August 1998 cruise missile strike on the El Shifa pharmaceutical plant in Sudan, part of the reprisals for the two embassy bombings earlier in the month, was justified based on the claim that the plant was producing precursors for chemical weapons, specifically for VX gas. The United States requested no inspection beforehand, and subsequent investigations showed that the claims were false. What is true is that the El Shifa plant produced over 50 percent of the pharmaceutical drugs used to combat the most deadly diseases facing the Sudanese, including malaria, tuberculosis, and cholera. It also produced almost all the veterinary medicine, in a country where much of the economy is dependent on animal husbandry. The plant made vital medicines available to the Sudanese at 20 percent of world market prices, a matter of life and death in a country with a per capita GNP of roughly $300 per year. One person was killed directly in the bombing, but the total number who died because of it (and because of the U.S.'s continuing stubborn insistence that it won't make any form of restitution) is presumably very high, in the thousands or tens of thousands.

In December of the same year, the United States conducted the Desert Fox bombing campaign against Iraq, because of a supposed lack of cooperation with UN weapons inspectors. It involved the killing of perhaps 1000 people and destruction of necessary infrastructure, including oil pipelines and even a grain depot. It was done to "degrade" Iraq's WMD capability and set it back from one to two years. It has made subsequent weapons inspections impossible — the United States withdrew inspectors before the bombing, and Iraq has refused to let any in since then. All responsible commentators, including Richard Butler, who was chief of UNSCOM, the UN Special Commission in charge of the weapons inspections, agree that the inspections were far more useful than the bombing in locating and destroying weapons of mass destruction in Iraq.

In fact, there is considerable evidence that before September 11 there were plans for another such attack, supposedly to degrade whatever weapons had been built up in almost three years without inspections. On February 16, 2001, there were strikes involving 50 planes on radar installations, some of them out of the aforementioned "no-fly zones." They were followed in August and early September of 2001 by at least six instances of pre-planned attacks to degrade Iraqi air defense. This was clearly part of a comprehensive plan for multiple strikes, with a U.S. government official quoted as saying, "Hitting targets one by one doesn't draw the same kind of attention or reaction. It takes longer, but it should eventually get the job done." George Friedman of Stratfor (a private military intelligence company) concluded that this sustained attack on Iraqi air defense was a prelude to another Desert Fox–style bombing.

This idea reached its height in December 2001 when the House International Affairs Committee considered a resolution declaring that "the refusal by Iraq to admit United Nations weapons inspectors into any facility covered by the provisions of Security Council Resolution 687 should be considered an act of aggression against the United States and its allies." A flurry of Internet-driven activism by the anti-sanctions movement helped prompt the committee to

change "act of aggression" to "growing threat," in which form the resolution
passed the House. In practice, it was simply a congressional attempt to legit-
imize for domestic consumption an idea that the executive branch had
already acted on numerous times. Why the possession of one of the two largest
arsenals of weapons of mass destruction in the world, along with a record of
using them (at Hiroshima and Nagasaki, for example), by the United States
does not constitute "aggression" against other countries was not addressed.

32. Reexamining National Security

The attacks of September 11 and the ensuing war on terrorism makes a reex-
amination of the concept of national security essential, since it will be at the
forefront of public discourse for some time to come.

Before September 11, it was impossible to use the phrase "national security" without an implied pair of quotes surrounding it. The deeply Orwellian
use of the term over the past half century had completely buried its literal
meaning. The United States is a national security state, which is to say a state
that supports a hypertrophied military and intelligence apparatus, justified by
the invocation of threats to national security. Since, between the Second
World War and September 11, there were no credible threats whatsoever to the
United States itself, this has not been an easy game to play.

The standard justification for keeping armed forces is defense against
external aggression. Very few would deny that this is a legitimate goal, and
only a few more would claim that most states can do without a self-defense
capability in the world we inhabit today. At a guess, a majority of the American public believes that the U.S. armed forces and military-intelligence-
industrial complex exists primarily for this purpose. This is a stunning victory
for official propaganda and newspeak. And yet the falsity of this belief should
be obvious. This country intervened with overwhelming force against the tiny
island of Grenada, with a staggering economic blockade against Cuba, hardly
daggers pointed at the heart of the United States. Ronald Reagan justified
attempts to destroy the Sandinistas by remarking on the fact that Nicaragua is
only two days' drive from Harlingen, Texas, conjuring an image of ravening
hordes of Nicaraguans overrunning Guatemala and Mexico to come boiling
up through our southern borders—this of a poor agricultural nation com-
posed mostly of landless peasants, which at the time of the Sandinista revolu-
tion had one working elevator. The Vietcong were hardly going to parachute

into Japan, much less the United States.

Against all these complete non-threats to the security of the United States, the government reacted with violence. And the jihadi networks involved in the September 11 attacks were largely created with U.S. funding, training, and arms. Although it's unclear whether bin Laden himself was on the CIA payroll, all the "Afghan Arabs" who came from far and wide to fight in their international jihad against one superpower were supported by the United States.

How do we understand a concept of self-defense that has seen the attempts of the Vietnamese, the Cubans, and the Nicaraguans for self-determination and freedom from foreign domination as a threat to our security, which we are justified in defending against with direct military force, but simultaneously created a genuine threat to our security against which we were unable to defend? Quite simply, "national security" has never since World War II been primarily about the safety of Americans, or even that of American allies. In government parlance, a threat to "national security" is a threat to elite interests, to the "pattern of relationships" ensuring the maintenance of U.S. global dominance that George Kennan talked about. Sometimes, protecting those interests is a threat to real national security, understood correctly as domestic safety. September 11 was an example of that. The war on Afghanistan may yet prove this again.

Rethinking national security is on the national agenda, and it must be on the agenda of any antiwar movement. In fact, in order to build a substantial antiwar movement, the domestic effects of war and militarism must be shown.

There are some obvious steps to be taken to ensure national security in this sense. The United States should stop supporting Israel's occupation of Palestine, end sanctions on Iraq, and sponsor an international peace conference designed to solve outstanding issues in the Middle East. The CIA should stop training extremist groups. The United States should stop selling arms around the world. The United States accounts for about half of total arms sales ($18.6 billion in 2000). A study in the mid-90s showed that the United States had supplied arms or military technology to parties in 39 of the then 42 active conflicts, being a major supplier in 18 of them. In 1999, it delivered $6.8 billion in arms to nations that violate the basic standards on human rights and democracy set out in the proposed International Code of Conduct on Arms Sales.

The United States has also severely compromised its national security and that of other nations by its attitude toward weapons of mass destruction — the basic idea being that the United States can have them and use them if it wants, without accountability, while nations in the Third World are accountable to the United States if they acquire them. This pattern is made clear in the Nuclear Non-Proliferation Treaty (NPT), for example. First proposed in 1968 by the United States, United Kingdom, and Soviet Union, it was a clear attempt to reserve to the existing nuclear powers the right to have nuclear weapons. Since other countries were unable to fathom the principled basis for this, there was considerable opposition until, as a sop, the original players threw in a clause about vertical proliferation, obligating existing powers to pursue disarmament, in addition to that about horizontal proliferation, keeping non-nuclear nations from going nuclear. A decade after the treaty was signed, the United States had over twice as many nuclear warheads as before.

This violation of treaty obligations by the United States played a critical role in the decision of countries like India not to sign the NPT. With India and Pakistan, both nuclear powers, on the brink of war as this is written, the U.S. strategy no longer seems very clever. It must be said, however, that there is an element of cultural supremacism in the frequent claims that there is risk of a nuclear exchange. India has explicitly renounced a first strike, something the United States has never done. Neither country has anything like the history of actual use of nuclear weapons on civilian populations and the general nuclear craziness that the United States has—Nixon seriously contemplated using nuclear weapons no less than four times. And, even so, the United States has refrained from use of nuclear weapons in recent conflicts (though use of tactical nuclear weapons was explicitly not ruled out in Afghanistan). Still, since the continued existence of nuclear weapons endangers everyone—the thought of Osama bin Laden getting his hands on one would give anyone the shivers—the only way to be safe is to get rid of all of them. Other countries will not do this unless the largest nuclear power, the United States, takes the lead.

33. Biological Weapons Again

Both because of the obvious threats of use by terrorists and because of their relevance with regard to Iraq and possibly other targets of the United States, it's useful to look at the question of biological weapons in greater depth.

In 1971, under considerable political pressure (and with the thought of the world's largest nuclear arsenal to fall back on), Richard Nixon announced a unilateral cessation of biological weapons research and destruction of existing weapons stocks. In direct contradiction to the logic constantly advocated by the proponents of the nuclear arms buildup, which stated that large arsenals were necessary as a bargaining position from which to get other countries to agree to disarmament, this unilateral disarmament rapidly led to a multilateral agreement to eliminate biological weapons. The Biological and Toxin Weapons Convention of 1972, signed now by 144 countries, called for the complete elimination of all such weapons. It was revealed in the 1990s that several countries, including the Soviet Union and Iraq, had violated this treaty. This was possible in part because the 1972 agreement had no verification and enforcement protocol, always seen as a necessity in any arms control agreement.

In 1995, countries embarked on a process to develop a comprehensive protocol allowing for mutual, intrusive inspections, culminating in a draft agreement in 2001, potentially a huge step toward a safer world. After years of foot-dragging, the United States announced suddenly, in July 2001, that it could not support such a protocol. Raising spurious concerns about the imperfection of negotiated protocols (it should go without saying that severe limitation, not absolute elimination, is the best that any arms control treaty can hope for and that said severe limitation is clearly better than a free-for-all), the United States claimed it would opt instead for espionage, bilateral agreements on export controls with allies, and the occasional unilateral enforcement measure—quite obviously no substitute for multilateral enforcement. In fact, some of those limits cited had been put there at U.S. insistence. For example, it consistently opposed regularly scheduled "transparency" inspections, which former Commerce Secretary William Daley claimed "offer no national security benefits."

In a telling indication of what national security really means to government policymakers, one of the concerns raised was that inspections might compromise proprietary material in the hands of biotech corporations, thus potentially harming their profits. This was raised even though, according to the Sunshine Project, a nonprofit arms-control think tank, this concern (presumably trivial in the face of the incredible threat of bio-weapons) could be adequately addressed within the context of the protocol.

Shortly thereafter, it was revealed in the New York Times (September 4) that existing U.S. bio-weapons research "pushes the limits" of the BTWC. Specifically mentioned were CIA programs that involved testing mock biological bombs and constructing a bio-weapons production facility in Nevada. As the Sunshine Project states in a news release (September 19), "If any other country conducted this research, it would have drawn harsh denunciations from the United States and quite possibly military attack." Perhaps even worse, this research was not disclosed in annual declarations of bio-defense activities (i.e., defense against biological warfare, legitimate under the BTWC), evading transparency mechanisms and raising serious questions about what the United States is really doing. As mentioned in a previous chapter, the scare caused by anthrax-laden letters helped to reveal that the United States is producing weapons-grade anthrax—it also has plans to genetically engineer a new strain of anthrax, ostensibly to test anthrax defense mechanisms.

After September 11, and specifically the anthrax scare, the Bush administration signaled that it might reconsider some kind of verification protocol, but wished to link this to evisceration of the central clause of the treaty. In place of an absolute prohibition on biological and toxin (toxins are poisons produced by living agents, like bacteria) weapons, the United States proposed to limit the prohibition to weapons of "lethal intent" against human beings, thus excluding agents that kill animals and crops (and can imperil humans by loss of livelihood and destruction of environment), such as Agent Green, a fungal agent proposed as a defoliant in Colombia and Afghanistan (radio transcripts indicate the Taliban knew of the plan and opposed it). It would also allow non-lethal, or supposedly non-lethal, weapons to be used on human beings, including proposed new crowd-control agents, first considered after the U.S. debacle in Somalia, and potentially also for use in anti-corporate-globalization mega-protests. On December 7, however, backpedaling to its previous position, it delivered what may have been the deathblow to the BTWC by again refusing to allow meaningful verification—a move that infuriated even its European allies.

All of this points up a larger concern in the whole recent U.S. approach to arms control. Instead of international treaties based on mutual cooperation, equal treatment of all states party to the agreement, and mutual inspections and verification procedures, the United States is moving more and more to asymmetric, unilateral (sometimes with close allies, sometimes without), and sometimes violent arms control methods. Those methods are not only more damaging than treaties, they are far less effective in addressing genuine security concerns.

With regard to the BTWC, in place of mutual inspection the United States proposes to rely on the so-called Australia Group, a secretive group of rich countries allied to the United States that has agreed on export controls of potential biological weapons material to other countries. Third World countries have complained that these controls, based on unpublished criteria, are arbitrary and unfair. This is very much part of a consistent pattern—the United States pretends to want arms reduction but in reality tries to reserve arms to itself and a small number of allies, consistently treating poor nations as enemies instead of allies in disarmament. This obviously undercuts the basis for those countries to cooperate genuinely, instead giving them an incentive to develop clandestine programs, thus greatly increasing security risks.

34. Containing the Rogue State

The difficulty the United States has with mutually binding treaties is just a tiny symptom of a much bigger problem — an overwhelming, overweening unilateralism that has the rest of the world aghast. The State Department likes to tout the concept of the rogue state (now called "states of concern"), states that have no regard for international law or the international community. Iraq always tops its list, and Libya, Syria, Sudan, and North Korea, among others, have been there as well. In reality, however, the chief rogue state is the United States itself.

The United States has an extraordinary history of violating international law, and some specific violations, such as the numerous wars of aggression and the targeting of civilian infrastructure, have been mentioned. The United States once even vetoed a Security Council resolution calling on states to obey international law — this was in 1986 after Nicaragua obtained a favorable ruling from the International Court of Justice in its case against the United States for the mining of Nicaragua's harbors and numerous other criminal acts during the 1980s (the United States never paid the $17 billion judgment). The United States also declares more or less openly that it does not consider itself bound by international treaties or by the decisions of international bodies vested with power to judge violations of international law. In fact, after the ICJ ruling the United States refused to recognize the authority of the ICJ — because of this, in a case brought against the United States and several of its NATO allies for the war on Serbia, the court was forced not to rule on the question of U.S. violation.

Similarly, even though the Security Council is the only body authorized to make war in the absence of a clear and immediate self-defense situation, the United States goes to the Security Council when it wishes and avoids it when it wishes. When it does use the Security Council, as with the Gulf War, it perverts its operation by using its economic power, its control of the IMF and World Bank, and other methods of coercion to influence decisions.

This attitude was most dramatically expressed in the attempts to establish an International Criminal Court, a permanent UN body to try individuals for war crimes, crimes of aggression, crimes against humanity, and genocide (the

ICJ only tries cases between nations). The United States was opposed to this on principle, simply because of the chance that an American might be tried by the court—it demanded as the price of its acceptance full immunity from war crimes for all Americans. Once the final treaty was completed, the vote for it was 120–7, as the United States joined the company of Israel, China, Libya, Iraq, Qatar, and Sudan.

Although Bill Clinton signed on to the treaty as a lame duck president, Republicans in the Senate want not just to stay out of the court, but also to destroy it. The American Service Members' Protection Act, endorsed by the Bush administration, would give the president the power to use military force against any country where U.S. personnel await trial by the ICC—leading many to dub it the "Invade the Hague Act."

Curtailing the unilateralism of the United States is an essential goal for progressive activists everywhere. There is a crying need for a democratic United Nations (right now a few countries hold all the power) with the power to enforce international law in an unbiased manner, with all states, even the United States, subject to it. Not only will that make the rest of the world more secure, it will increase security in the United States by removing perhaps the single biggest source of resentment against the United States— its imperial arrogance.

Many people have called the war on terrorism the new Cold War. The similarity is based not on material and structural factors, but on the ideological means by which foreign and domestic policies are justified. There, as here, there is a supposedly global enemy that can always be invoked, no matter where one fights. When no evidence could be found that Hanoi took orders from Moscow, American policymakers theorized that Hanoi was so trusted by Moscow that no orders need be given—similarly, here, if attacking some organization, especially in the Islamic world, suits U.S. strategic interests, the lack of a link to al-Qaeda will simply be a sign that the link is buried very deep. Again, here is an enemy one can genuinely conjure with, one that actually poses a far more significant threat to the safety of Americans than the Soviet Union ever did, and much more suitable to the role than the drug traffickers and isolated rogue states of the early 90s-era search for new enemies.

It is still too early to tell whether this war on terrorism will genuinely usher in a new era, but it is certainly possible. Like corporate globalization, the war on terrorism may become a major continuing theme in the spreading of U.S.

and First World dominance over the planet. Obviously, corporate globalization has much larger scope, but the military underpinning of economic domination is essential to that domination, and that is largely what the war on terrorism will be about.

More insight into the potential future effects of the war on terrorism can be gained by analyzing Bush's State of the Union address, delivered on January 29, 2002. The tone set was distressingly reminiscent of the first Cold War, of the 1950s and the early 1960s. According to this address, we are once again a beacon of civilization, on a higher moral plane than others, opposing absolute evil—in addition to Bush's two references to the "civilized world," mentioned earlier, we learn that Iran, Iraq, and North Korea, along with their "terrorist allies," constitute an "axis of evil." In a stunning display of hypocrisy, Bush even indicted Iraq for attempting to weaponize anthrax, something the United States has been doing itself. We assert as forcefully as we did in the days of fighting the "international Communist conspiracy" that the war on terrorism allows us to intervene wherever we like, if we so choose—"some governments will be timid in the face of terror. And make no mistake: If they do not act, America will." Once again, any development anywhere is a threat to our national security, and "all nations should know: America will do what is necessary to ensure our nation's security."

We need permanently higher military budgets in order to "defend" ourselves (with useless and expensive high-tech programs like missile defense and the joint-strike fighter, not with ways to defend against realistic terrorist attacks), another throwback to the 1950s—"My budget includes the largest increase in defense spending in two decades, because while the price of freedom and security is high, it is never too high: whatever it costs to defend our country, we will pay it." Bush's proposed new military budget is $379 billion, an increase of $48 billion over the already unexpectedly high 2001 budget— the increase alone is larger than any other nation's military budget.

We are once again beset by internal enemies—"And as government works to better secure our homeland, America will continue to depend on the eyes and ears of alert citizens." This is not yet at the level of the House Un-American Activities Committee hearings and pamphlets on how to tell if your neighbor is a Communist that characterized the 1950s, but it is a significant step closer.

Our "economic security" is essential to our national security, so disagreements on economic policy and on how high corporate profit should be must be submerged in an artificial national unity. Congress must pass an energy policy that involves more drilling for oil in the United States, must give the president trade promotion authority (popularly known as "fast-track") in concluding "free trade" agreements, and must make the Bush tax cut permanent—all in the name of security.

We are called once again to sacrifice for a very particularly conceived "national good"—"My call tonight is for every American to commit at least two years—4,000 hours over the rest of your lifetime—to the service of your neighbors and your nation." The newly created USA Freedom Corps needs volunteers to help preserve our "homeland security." The call for citizens to do some form of public service, in itself, is not a bad thing, but the choice to ask them to prepare for possible terrorist attacks instead of trying to provide education, housing, and social services to people who need them is about attempting to mobilize the time and energy of the people in the service of the existing power structure and about co-opting other kinds of popular mobilization.

In sum, the war on terrorism will involve more frequent military interventions, with less of an attempt to placate international sensibilities, and with the constant excuse of protecting American security. It will involve more overt appeals to Western cultural supremacy, although couched in universalist terms like "the rule of law, limits on the power of the state, respect for women, private property, free speech, equal justice and religious tolerance." It will involve more arms proliferation and a growth of military spending, and a lessening of democracy in this country, both in terms of the public's ability to affect decisions and in terms of individual freedom to dissent from the course advocated by dominant institutions.

But this is far from the whole story. Excess inevitably produces a reaction and empires sooner or later overreach themselves. It is quite possible that, looking back, September 11 will be seen as the turning point for the American Empire. Ever since the publication in 1941 of a famous article by Harry Luce, founder of *Life* magazine, the twentieth century has been described as the American century. Many in the elite here in the United States drew from that century the lesson that there was no limit to American imperial reach and that world rule by a judicious combination of force, economic control, and mass propaganda could really be established without adverse consequences to that elite. And, in fact, as has often been noted, the Western imperial project was an ideal way to "export" the inherent contradictions of a society and a world of gross inequality, based more and more solely on the profit motive, to a place, the Third World, where they could easily be dealt with.

The lesson of the twenty-first century has already been made abundantly clear. This will be the century of "blowback," the century where the predictable consequences of constantly multiplying contradictions and increasing social strains will necessarily affect even the elite in the heart of the empire. Unless something drastic is done, the constantly increasing level of production and consumption of resources will lead to a global environmental collapse, and to depletion of vital nonrenewable resources. The lack of any concerted attempt to address diseases like AIDS, a mere epiphenomenon of a society based on profit instead of human needs, may well lead to a century of super-plagues. And, as September 11 showed, even in the field of foreign policy, where the United States has such a seemingly overwhelming advantage in power, further attempts at aggression and domination may well carry within themselves the seeds of their own destruction and of backlash. The war on terrorism is likely to be the primary arena where this will play out, although perhaps not the only one.

Simultaneously, the war on terrorism also greatly increases the potential fruitfulness of progressive activism. Like corporate globalization, it is one of those threads that show the interconnectedness of far-flung events to each other and to our daily lives in the United States. The insanity of continuing on the militarist path we are now on is made newly evident. When past military actions and current policies are creating such profound reservoirs of resentment, to continue to proliferate arms, commit military aggression, and create the potential for ever more and ever more harmful assaults is clearly senseless. We continue to multiply the complexity and vulnerability of our society, not just with nuclear power plants but, as we are now irremediably aware, even with skyscrapers, while simultaneously letting pressing social problems fester and even exacerbating them — clearly something that will affect even the American middle class, invading their hitherto privileged and sheltered existence. September 11 forced us to recognize that we are of the world, and the potential to make clear to people that they cannot profit by allowing our government to continue fouling that world has never been greater.

The war on terrorism has placed our nation and our national character on the proving ground. There is still a real question about what America will be — both in its own eyes and the world's. This is a deeply ambiguous country. Some around the world think of American values — individual rights, democracy, the rule of law, the right to self-determination, due process — as simply a cloak for imperial self-interest, and, as we have seen, there is some justice in their thinking that. Simultaneously, however, those principles have been a beacon to other peoples. They have given inspiration — Ho Chi Minh, in 1945, read the Declaration of Independence over the radio to the nation of

Vietnam, newly free of French and Japanese domination. They have given direction—many learned from those principles what they should be fighting for, often against the United States and its clients. They are part of the basis of the Charter of the United Nations, whose first clause reads, "We the People of the United Nations," and of the Universal Declaration of Human Rights.

At home, we are the country of blind support for the president and his war-mongering, of "Nuke Afghanistan," and of hate crimes in the wake of September 11. We are also the nation of people spontaneously organizing to defend Arab-Americans against hate crimes and getting past their personal grief to build an antiwar movement. In a particular testament both to the nobility of some Americans and to the possibilities of a different kind of world, some family members of victims of September 11 attacks have traveled to Afghanistan, in a tour dubbed "From one Ground Zero to another Ground Zero," and met with Afghan families who have lost loved ones in the U.S. attacks—in hopes of helping to foster deeper human bonds as they all struggle with their losses inflicted by those that seem to share a callous disregard for human life. Some are beginning to see that we are connected more to Afghan peasants, in our shared vulnerability, than to any of the people with the fingers on the triggers—the terrorists or the man in the White House.

Nothing is yet written in stone. The future is what we make of it. To make that better vision of America real will require ceaseless struggle, but so does anything worthwhile.

NOTES

Part One

1   UNICEF report, August 1999.
2   Gar Alperovitz, *The Decision to Drop the Atomic Bomb: The Architecture of an American Myth* (New York: Knopf, 1995).
3   *LA Weekly*, September 21–27, 2001.
4   *Washington Post*, December 7, 2001.
5   *Washington Post*, October 30, 2001.
6   *St. Petersburg Times*, November 1, 2001
7   BBC, September 18, 2001. http://news.bbc.co.uk/hi/english/world/south_asia/newsid_1550000/1550366.stm
8   Netaid, Online Action on Extreme Poverty, http://app.netaid.org/WhatWorks/1.2.html?pillar_id=4&proj_id=99
9   *New York Times*, September 28, 2001.
10 Op. cit.
11 Geoff Simons, *The Scourging of Iraq: Sanctions, Law, and Natural Justice* (New York: St. Martin's Press, 1996).
12 Op. cit., p. 115.
13 Washingtonpost.com, Dot.Mil column, William Arkin, November 4, 2001.
14 *Independent, London*, December 9, 2001.
15 *New York Times*, November 30, 2001.
16 *Financial Times*, November 21, 2001.
17 Collateral Damage Made Real, Deborah James, Alternet, http://www.alternet.org/story.html?StoryID=12077
18 *Guardian, London*, December 10, 2001.
19 *Toronto Star*, December 4, 2001.
20 BBC, December 11, 2001, http://news.bbc.co.uk/hi/english/world/south_asia/newsid_1703000/1703770.stm.
21 Reuters, December 6, 2001.
22 Reuters, December 12, 2001.
23 BBC, January 9, 2002, http://news.bbc.co.uk/hi/english/world/south_asia/newsid_1750000/1750645.stm
24 *The Guardian*, January 3, 2002, "Refugees left in the cold at 'slaughterhouse' camp" http://www.guardian.co.uk/Archive/Article/0,4273,4328292,00.html
25 Pentagon spokesperson Victoria Clarke, to the press, December 10, 2001.
26 Department of Defense briefing, October 15, 2001.
27 Marc W. Herold, "A Dossier on Civilian Victims of United States' Aerial Bombing of Afghanistan: A Comprehensive Accounting," Forthcoming.

28 Human Rights Watch press release, October 30, 2001.

29 *Toronto Globe & Mail*, November 3, 2001.

30 Human Rights Watch backgrounder on cluster bombs, October 2001.

31 Herold.

32 Federation of American Scientists http://www.fas.org/man/dod-101/sys/dumb/blu-82.htm.

33 Herold.

34 Herold.

35 Department of Defense briefing, November 19, 2001.

36 *Washington Post*, December 11, 2001.

37 Gary Webb, *Dark Alliance: The CIA, the Contras, and the Crack Cocaine Explosion* (New York: Seven Stories Press, 1998).

38 *Christian Science Monitor*, October 5, 2001.

39 Congressional testimony, December 6, 2001.

40 *New York Times*, October 24, 2001.

41 ACLU report, http://www.aclu.org/congress/l102301j.html

42 ACLU press release, December 5, 2001.

43 *Washington Post*, November 16, 2001.

44 *Washington Post*, October 21, 2001.

45 *Los Angeles Times*, November 8, 2001.

46 *Newsweek*, November 5, 2001.

47 Human Rights World Watch Report 2001. http://www.hrw.org/wr2k1/usa/

48 ACLU letter and memorandum to members of Congress. http://www.aclu.org/congress/l112901a.html

49 Senate Judiciary Committee, December 6, 2001.

50 *Village Voice*, December 12–18, 2001.

51 Gallup Poll, December 9, 1999. http://www.gallup.com/poll/releases/pr991209.asp

52 Gallup Poll, September 2001, reported in *Boston Globe*, September 30, 2001.

53 *Chicago Tribune*, September 13, 2001.

54 David Horowitz, "Open Letter to Antiwar Demonstrators," run as a paid ad in college newspapers.

55 Salon.com, The prime-time smearing of Sami al-Arian, January 19, 2002, http://www.salon.com/tech/feature/2002/01/19/bubba/

56 *St. Petersburg Times*, December 20, 2001, http://www.sptimes.com/News/122001/TampaBay/USF_will_fire_Al_Aria.shtml.

57 *St. Petersburg Times*, December 22, 2001, http://www.sptimes.com/News/122201/TampaBay/Critics_of_Al_Arian_f.shtml.

58 FAIR Action Alert, November 2, 2001.

59 *Der Spiegel*, http://www.spiegel.de/politik/ausland/0,1518,158625,00.html (in German).

60 *Chicago Tribune*, October 22, 2001, reported in SoundBites, Extra! November-December 2001.

61 *David Letterman Show*, CBS, October 10, 2001.

62 *Extra!* November/December 2001.

63 FAIR Action Alert, October 2, 2001.

64 *Washington Post*, September 26, 2001.

65 *Los Angeles Times*, November 4, 2001.

66 Agence France-Presse, November 17, 2001.

67 *Fox News Special Report* with Brit Hume, November 5, 2001.

68 *Los Angeles Times*, December 2, 2001.

69 *Independent*, UK, December 4, 2001.

70 *Los Angeles Times*, November 24, 2001, reported in Herold.

71 Pentagon press briefing, December 4, 2001, reported in Pentagon Denials and Civilian Death in Afghanistan, David Corn, Alternet, http://www.alternet.org/story.html?StoryID=12044

72 *New York Times*, November 23, 2001, reported in FAIR Action Alert, December 12, 2001.

73 *CBS Evening News*, December 1, 2001, reported in FAIR Action Alert, December 12, 2001.

74 *CBS Evening News*, October 23, 2001.

75 FAIR Action Alert, December 12, 2001.

76 *Washington Post*, October 31, 2001.

77 *New York Times*, November 1, 2001, reported in FAIR Action Alert, November 1, 2001.

78 FAIR Action Alert, November 8, 2001.

79 FAIR Action Alert, October 12, 2001.

80 *Guardian*, London, October 17, 2001.

81 Op. cit.

82 *Washington Post*, December 6, 2001.

83 Op. cit.

84 Pentagon press briefing, October 22, 2001.

85 *ABC This Week*, October 28, 2001, reported in SoundBites, Extra! November/December 2001.

86 *New York Times*, October 28, 2001.

87 Rumsfeld interview with al-Jazeera, October 16, 2001, http://www.defenselink.mil/news/Oct2001/t10172001_t1016sd.html.

88 CNN, October 3, 2001.

89 The CNN of the Arab World, Tamara Straus, Alternet, http://www.alternet.org/story.html?StoryID=11811

90 *Washington Post*, November 13, 2001.

91 Gallup International poll, September 14–17, 2001. http://www.gallup-international.com/terrorismpoll_figures.htm

92 *USA Today*, October 1, 2001, reporting on a poll published September 19, 2001.

93 *The Nation*, October 29, 2001.

Part Two

1 *National Review*, October 15, 2001.

2 *Wall Street Journal*, October 9, 2001.

3 *New York Times Week in Review*, June 13, 1999.

4 "Allied Air War Struck Broadly in Iraq: Officials Admit Strategy Went Beyond Purely Military Targets," *Washington Post*, June 23, 1991.

5 Bob Woodward, *Shadow*, cited in Consortium News, Behind Colin Powell's Legend, http://www.consortiumnews.com/2000/122600b.html

6 "The Secret Behind the Sanctions: How the US Intentionally Destroyed Iraq's Water Supply," *The Progressive*, August 10, 2001, Thomas Nagy. The documents can be found on the Web in the National Security Archive, http://www.gwu.edu/~nsarchiv by keyword searches.

7 *Washington Post*, June 23, 1991.

8 *Le Nouvel Observateur* (France), interview, January 15–21, 1998, p. 76.

9 Stephen Shalom, "Gravy Train: Feeding the Pentagon by Feeding Somalia," Z *Magazine*, February 1993, revised version on the Web at http://www.zmag.org/ZMag/articles/shalomsomalia.html

10 William Maynes Charles, "Relearning Intervention," *Foreign Policy*, 68 (Spring 1995) .

11 Phyllis Bennis, *Calling the Shots: How Washington Dominates Today's UN*, 2nd ed. (New York: Olive Branch Press, July 2000) p. 250.

12 See "The U.S. and Genocide in Rwanda," National Security Archive, http://www.gwu.edu/~nsarchiv/NSAEBB/NSAEBB53/press.html

13 For good accounts of the history of the sanctions, see: Dilip Hiro, *Neighbors, Not Friends: Iraq and Iran after the Gulf Wars* (London: Routledge, 2001); Sarah Graham-Brown, *Sanctioning Saddam: The Politics of Intervention in Iraq* (London: I B Tauris, 1999); Geoff Simons, *The Scourging of Iraq: Sanctions, Law, and Natural Justice* (New York: St. Martin's Press, 1996).

Part Three

1 Cited in Alexander Cockburn, "Killing with Smaller Stones," http://www.workingforchange.com/article.cfm?ItemId=12602

2 To understand the Oslo process and the Israel/Palestine issue, see Noam Chomsky, *The Fateful Triangle*, 2nd ed. (Sydney: Pluto Press, 2000).

3 *Baltimore Sun*, December 12, 2001.

4 Cited in William Blum, "Follow the Changing Story: Atta, The *Times* and the Iraqi Agent," http://www.counterpunch.org/blumatta.html

5 Andrew and Patrick Cockburn, *Out of the Ashes: The Resurrection of Saddam Hussein* (New York: HarperCollins, 1999), p. 37.

6 "ABC News Peter Jennings Special", February 7, 1998.

7 *New York Times*, Thomas Friedman, July 7, 1991.

8 *Washington Post*, May 16, 2001.

9 *The Economist*, February 24, 2001.

10 Human Rights Watch, August 2000 http://www.hrw.org/press/2000/08/iraq0804.htm

11 UN Secretary-General's report, May 18, 2001, para., 129. http://www.un.org/Depts/oip/reports/S2001_505.pdf

12 *Daily Telegraph*, February 21, 2001.

13 Speech, March 8, 2001.

14 Noam Chomsky, *Deterring Democracy*, Hill and Wang, on the Web, chapter 5, Segment 4 http://www.zmag.org/chomsky/dd/dd-c05-s04.html

INDEX

assassination, 17, 55, 57, 129
Associated Press, 54
Atta, Mohammed, 131
Australia Group, 142
axis of evil, 145
AZT (AIDS drug), 109

Baker, James, 106
Banzer Suarez, Hugo, 56
Bayer corporation, 61
BBC (British Broadcasting Corporation), 83
Berkeley (California), 76–77
bin Laden, Osama, 33, 41, 53, 83, 111; CIA
    and, 58, 139; extradition of, 21; Islamic world
    support for, 57, 96; role in 9/11 attacks, 16, 28,
    29–30; video response of, 14, 15, 18, 89
Bin Laden: The Forbidden Truth (Bristard and
    Dasquie), 33
Biological and Toxin Weapons Convention
    (1972), 22, 131, 141, 142
biological weapons, 107, 131, 140–43. See also
    anthrax scare
Blair, Tony, 29
bombing campaigns, 115. See also Afghanistan;
    Gulf War; Iraq; Serbia; Vietnam
bombs: cluster, 45–47, 49; nuclear, 14–15, 59,
    136, 140; smart, 43–44. See also weapons
Boucher, Richard, 37
Bradol, Jean-Hervé, 36
Brazil, 108
Bristard, Jean-Charles, 33
Britain, 20–21, 29, 113, 130; in colonial India,
    100–101; role in Afghanistan war, 36, 41, 52,
    93; sanctions plan for Iraq, 133–34. See also
    United Kingdom
Brown v. Board of Education (1954), 73
Brzezinski, Zbygniew, 110
Burman, Tony, 83
Bush, George, Sr., 18, 105–6, 132, 133
Bush, George W., 27, 29, 131–32, 145; on bin
    Laden's guilt, 30; military tribunal order of,
    70; post 9/11 speech, 11, 13, 16–19
Bush administration, 41, 59, 61, 90, 127; and
    arms control treaties, 142; and bombing of
    Afghanistan, 33–34; reluctance to negotiate,
    26, 29, 30, 31; on rights of terrorists, 65,
    70–71; unilateralism of, 22, 23
Butler, Richard, 137

Carter administration, 57–58
Caspian Sea oil, 32–33, 125
Castro, Fidel, 57
CBS news, 85
censorship of media, 83, 86–89, 91–92
Central Asia, 32–33, 111, 125
Chamberlain, Neville, 12
Chechnya war, 55
Cheney, Lynne, 78
ChevronTexaco corporation, 64
child mortality: in Afghanistan, 36, 75; in Iraq,
    9–10, 14, 118, 119; Palestinian, 14
children, schooling of, 73, 109
Chile, 95, 104
China, 24, 55, 59, 136
Chomsky, Noam, 32
Chowkar-Karez (Afghan village), 45
Christian Aid, 35, 40
Christian fundamentalists, 19
Church Commission, 57–58, 66
CIA (Central Intelligence Agency), 14, 133, 139,
    141; in Afghanistan, 52, 110; congressional
    investigation of, 57–58, 66
Cipla (Indian drug company), 61, 108
Cipro (antibiotic), 61, 64
civilian casualties, 18, 19, 87, 115–16; in
    Afghanistan, 41, 44–51; genocidal, 74–75, 104,
    114; in Iraq, 117, 130, 137; in Israeli-Palestinian
    conflict, 56, 128–29; in Kosovo, 114, 115;
    media coverage of, 83–86, 117; in Sudan, 137;
    in Vietnam, 97, 117. See also child mortality
civilian infrastructure destruction: in
    Afghanistan, 44, 47–48; in Iraq, 105, 106–7;
    in Serbia, 114. See also Geneva Convention
civil rights restrictions, 65–71; of immigrants,
    66–68, 71
Clear Channel Communications, 77
Clinton, Bill, 120, 121–22, 144
Clinton administration, 67, 132
cluster bombs (CBU-87), 45–47, 49
CNN (Cable News Network), 80, 85, 88, 91, 92
Cold War, 104, 144–45
collateral damage, 116, 117. See also civilian
    casualties
colonialism, 99–101, 102, 123; undoing, 14, 104
Constant, Emanuel, 17, 55
Cooksey, John, 74
corporate globalization, 103, 144–45

justice, 19, 31
justification of (military) force, 104, 116
just war, principles of, 94–95, 115–16

Karzai, Hamid, 124
Kashmir (India), 55
Kazakhstan, 32
Keegan, John, 52
Kelly, Michael, 82
Kennan, George, 102, 139
Kennedy, Robert, 68
Khalilzad, Zalmay, 124
Khatami, Mohammad, 7
Kipling, Rudyard, 99–100, 101
Kissinger, Henry, 17, 55
Kosovo war, 29, 88, 94, 112–14, 115
Krauthammer, Charles, 20
Krugman, Paul, 64
Kuwait invasion, 12, 27, 28, 46, 133. See also
    Gulf War

landmines, 34–35, 46
Late Victorian Holocausts (Davis), 101
Latin America, 55–56, 104
Lee, Barbara, 62, 76
licensing of drugs, 61, 108
Lockhead Martin corporation, 59
London Daily Telegraph, 52, 134
Los Angeles Times, 82, 84
Lowry, Richard, 100
Luce, Harry, 146
Lumumba, Patrice, 57

Mafia/mobsters, 32, 68
Maher, Bill, 76
Malaysia, 97
Martin, David, 85
massacre of civilians. See civilian casualties
massacre of prisoners, 51–52, 54
Mayan Indians, 56
McCain, John, 11
McKinley, William, 100
media, 12, 48, 54, 79–86, 114; Arabic television,
    86, 87, 89–81, 92; censorship of, 83, 86–89,
    91–92; on civilian deaths, 83–86, 117;
    coverage of antiwar views by, 81–83; foreign,
    45, 83, 84, 88; freedom of, 90, 91–92;
    hate campaigns by, 77; and public opinion,

93; warmongering by, 31, 79–81
medicine in Iraq, 107. See also drugs
Middle East, 10, 105, 106, 135. See also
    specific country
Miklaszewski, Jim, 85
military force, authorization of, 21–22.
    See also US military
military tribunal order, 70
Mine Ban Treaty (1997), 46
Mineta, Norman, 61
Moro Islamic Liberation Front, 126
Morris, Thomas L., 64
Morrow, Lance, 11, 12
Moussaoi, Zacarias, 70
multilateralism, 22–26
Musharraf, Pervez, 25, 30, 37
Muslims, racial profiling of, 72–74. See also
    Islamic world; Taliban
Mutawakil, Wakil Ahmed, 7
Muttaqi, Amir Khan, 30
My Lai massacre (Vietnam), 117

Naik, Niaz, 33
National Missile Defense program (US), 22, 59
National Review (magazine), 73, 100
national security, 67, 138–40, 141, 145
NATO (North Atlantic Treaty Organization),
    23; occupation of Kosovo by, 28–29, 113;
    war on Serbia, 44, 89, 100, 112, 113–14, 143
Nazi Holocaust, 104
necessity principle, in war, 94
negotiation, 21, 28, 30. See also diplomacy
neocolonialism, 102, 123. See also colonialism
new Cold War, 144–45
new McCarthyism, 78
newspapers, 81–82. See also specific newspapers
New World Order, 18, 102
New York Times, 64, 80, 82, 86, 100, 131, 141
Nicaragua, 38, 58, 95, 104, 138, 143
Nixon, Richard, 140
Northern Alliance, 41, 51–52, 54–55
North Korea, 145
no-tell searches, 65
Nuclear Non-Proliferation Treaty, 140
nuclear weapons, 14–15, 59, 136, 140
Observer (newspaper), 93
Oil for Food program, 119, 120–22, 134, 135
oil pipeline, 32–33, 111, 125

Schneider, Rene, 17
School of the Americas, 55–56
schools, 73, 109
Schumer, Charles, 13
Schwarzkopf, Norman, 132
searches, no-tell, 65
secret evidence, 67
security concerns, 56–61; airport security, 60–61. See also national security
self-defense, 19–22, 136, 139, 143
September 11th attacks, 7–8, 58, 131; as attack on freedom, 13?, 65; bin Laden's role in, 29; and Pearl Harbor compared, 11–12; reactions to, 15
Serbia, 28–29, 110; NATO bombing of, 9, 44, 49, 112, 113–14; NATO war against, 75, 100, 143
Shadow (Woodward), 105
Shapiro, Neal, 87
Sharon, Ariel, 14, 128, 129–30
Short, Clare, 41
shura (assembly of Islamic clerics), 28, 29
Siad Barre, Mohammed, 111, 112
smart bombs, 43–44
smart sanctions for Iraq, 133–35
smuggling in Iraq, 135, 136
Snowcroft, Brent, 132, 133
solidarity and patriotism, 62
Somalia, 111–12, 125–26
Sontag, Susan, 76
South Africa, 9, 108
Soviet Union, 15, 24, 110, 136, 141, 144.
    See also Russia
Spann, Johnny "Mike," 52
Sponeck, Hans von, 130, 135
Stahl, Leslie, 9–10, 99
Star Wars, 59
state-sponsored terrorism, 14, 54–56
Stocking, Barbara, 36
Stufflebeem, John, 39
Sudan, 9, 136–37
suicide bombings, 129
Sullivan, Andrew, 76
Sunshine Project (think tank), 141
Syria, 59

Taliban, 28, 41, 83, 110, 125; advent of, 54; Bush's demands of, 16–17, 29; CIA support of, 58; and food aid, 37, 38–40; foreign fighters in,

51, 52; and humanitarian crisis, 43; media savvy of, 88; Pakistan's support for, 24; prisoners, 54; radio propaganda and, 89; US negotiation with, 21, 30, 33, 111
terrorism, 9; domestic, 66; justice for, 96; long-term solutions to, 97; philosophy of, 10; state-sponsored, 14, 54–56; UN resolution against, 21–22, 25. See also war on terrorism
terrorists: networks, 96, 126; and racial profiling, 72; rights of, 53–54, 65–71; training camps, 16, 29, 55–56; US harboring of, 17–18
Third World, 100–103, 109, 114, 116–17; and arms control, 142–43; corporate interests in, 102, 103; elites of, 110, 123; hatred of U.S. by, 13–14; as new white man's burden, 100, 101; US domination of, 97, 146. See also specific countries
Thomas, Bill, 63
ticking-bomb situation, 69
Tora Bora attacks, 85
torture, 54, 55–56, 68–69
trade promotion authority, 62–63
Turkey, 132
Turkmenistan, 32
Turner, Jim, 84
Tutsi-Hutu rivalry (Rwanda), 114

Uigur separatists, 55
unilateralism, US, 22, 23, 24, 32, 95, 98; future of, 142, 144
Union Carbide corporation, 18
United Kingdom, 25, 132, 133–34. See also Britain
United Nations: Charter of, 20, 22, 23, 31, 148; Compensation Fund, 119, 135; Convention Against Torture, 69; Development Program, 124; food aid from, 37; High Commission for Refugees, 35; need for democracy in, 144; Office for the Coordination of Humanitarian Affairs, 35; peacekeepers, 114; sanctions on Afghanistan, 111; sanctions on Iraq, 14, 118–19; Security Council resolutions, 20–22, 23–25, 118, 143; weapons inspectors, 137
UNICEF, 14, 35, 36, 119
United States: and arms control treaties, 141; cultural supremacism of, 8, 140, 146; domination of Middle East by, 10, 135; economic domination of, 23–24, 31–32, 33,